OUTSOURCING
Avoiding Unnecessary Adversities

Vick P. Dini

Cataloging-in-Publication Data

Dini, Vick P.

    Outsourcing: Avoiding Unnecessary Adversities
    p. cm.
    Includes index and bibliographical references.
    1. Contracting out. 2. Corporate governance. I. Title.

ISBN-13: 978-1-0897-2649-4

First printing released in 2020

Cover design by Ginaris Sarra

To my parents Ana and Pier.
Although separated by the crisis,
we're always together in our hearts.

ACKNOWLEDGEMENTS

I would like to thank everyone who supported me in conducting this field project. Foremost, my tutor, Professor Elena Cantù, whose advice guided me throughout the prosecution of this endeavor and contributed to its qualitative amelioration. I would also like to thank Professor Paola Mariani, who offered us her help and care throughout this Second Level Specializing Master in Corporate Governance and whom I very much esteem. Thanks to all the anonymous interviewees who participated in this research and were instrumental in constructing the empirical and practical foundations upon which the proposed toolkit was built.

Thanks to Professor Antonella Occhino, Professor Serena Manzin, and Professor Alfonso Del Giudice, among all the other professors who shared their knowledge and favored our academic growth.

Thanks to my family and friends who encouraged me in times of difficulty and whose suggestions were certainly found useful.

Finally, I would like to thank all the authors of the works included in the List of References, for the time and effort they dedicated to such ventures and for making their knowledge public.

TABLE OF CONTENTS

LIST OF TABLES

LIST OF FIGURES

ABSTRACT

OUTSOURCING: AVOIDING UNNECESSARY ADVERSITIES

Author: Vick Pierce Dini
Tutor: Elena Cantù

Milan, November 2018

The main objective of this field project was to propose a toolkit for outsourcing that helps avoid unnecessary adversities, while being compatible with the ISO 37500:2014. For this purpose, a qualitative research was conducted, consisting of a literature review and an empirical analysis. The former embodied eight recent case studies, while the latter, several semi-structured interviews. Successively, the results and findings were taken into consideration while preparing the toolkit, which comprises methodologies, frameworks, tools, and techniques that might help prevent the detected adversities.

Keywords: case study, corporate strategy, corporate governance, empirical research, family business, ISO 37500, outsourcing failures, SME

INTRODUCTION

This field project is about outsourcing and its main purpose is to help avoid unnecessary adversities throughout endeavors of this kind, by proposing a toolkit that is compatible with the international outsourcing standard ISO 37500, released in 2014, and is backed by a qualitative research, which consisted of a literature review and an empirical analysis.

Although it was first identified as a business strategy in 1989 (Mullin, 1996, p. 29), outsourcing is still retained a valid sourcing strategy. Currently, the Oxford Dictionaries define it as the obtention of "(goods or a service) from an outside or foreign supplier, especially in place of an internal source[, or to] contract (work) out or abroad" (Outsource, n.d.).

Despite the fact that much has been written on this topic, the relatively recent release of the aforementioned standard, in addition to the author's related work experience, motivated him to further delve into this matter and contribute to science by:

1. Compiling and synthesizing a compendium of eight of the latest case studies about failed outsourcing initiatives;

2. Conducting, and revealing the findings of, an interview-based empirical analysis on this subject; and

3. Proposing a toolkit to help avoid unnecessary outsourcing adversities, gathered from the previous couple of points.

Therefore, this document has been structured in the following manner, taking best practices into account:

- Chapter I, *The Problem*, presents the problem statement, main and specific objectives, assumptions, delimitations, limitations, and the justification of this project.

- Chapter II, *Reference Framework*, is composed of a conceptual framework, which contains those concepts deemed necessary for the comprehension of this document, and a theoretical framework, with eight case studies and the methodologies, frameworks, tools, and techniques that were included in the toolkit (Chapter V).

- Chapter III, *Methodological Framework*, delves into the methodology that was followed and the steps taken to achieve the objectives.

- Chapter IV, *Results*, reveals the findings of the empirical analysis.

- Chapter V, *Toolkit*, presents a set of methodologies, frameworks, tools, and techniques that will hopefully help avoid unnecessary outsourcing adversities.

- *Conclusions* and *Recommendations* present the conclusions that were reached throughout the project and offer recommendations for further research.

CHAPTER I
THE PROBLEM

I.1. Problem Statement

With the advent of globalization and the Internet, the competition among companies has continually intensified year after year, with some of them even becoming cannibalistic. Hence, most boards of directors have developed strategies which are strongly oriented towards cost-reduction and flexibility, in order to adapt to globally ever-changing customer bases and market demand and offering.

An evident consequence and irrefutable proof of current high levels of corporate competitiveness is what the media of the United States of America call the "Retail Apocalypse," referring to the preponderant rise of e-commerce since 2010, led by Amazon, and the desolation and inevitable closure of traditional brick-and-mortar retail stores, such as Gap, J. C. Penney, Kmart, Macy's, Sears, Toys "R" Us, and Walgreens. Moreover, Noah Smith enunciates a possible, yet astounding, side effect of this market trend: the dollars would be "spent online, and the money would flow to the people working for Amazon in big cities - increasing demand for life in those places, while leaving everywhere else to rot" (Sen & Smith, 2018). Likewise, in the United Kingdom companies such as Homebase, Marks and Spencer, Mothercare, and

Poundworld are facing the "End of the High Street" (Martin, 2018). According to Berg (as cited in ITV, 2018), "In retail today, if you don't differentiate from your rivals; if you're not relevant to your customers you don't stand a chance. This is retail Darwinism, you evolve or die."

As if inter-company competition weren't already tough enough, many companies have been competing with themselves for decades. This intra-company competition is also referred to as "corporate cannibalism" and has proven useful as a means to increase the company's overall market share in particularly stagnant markets, even if it leads to reducing that of each of its products individually (Hindle, 2008). Diageo, Nestlé, Unilever, and Procter & Gamble (P&G) are influential multi-brand, multinational corporations, among which the latter is of particular interest, as it has dealt with planned cannibalization for almost a century and also pioneered "brand management."

After acquiring Gillette in 2005, P&G's innovative push and expertise led to the creation of the Gillette Guard, a custom-made razor for the newly targeted, low-income Indian consumers. This product uses 80% fewer parts than the already top-selling Gillette Vector and was priced at less than 3% of the higher-end Gillette Fusion ProGlide. As a matter of fact, nearly six months after its launch in 2010, the Guard had captured over 50% of the Indian razor market share. The logic behind this strategic move is that it was better to anticipate a disruptive competitor, who'd take a chunk of P&G's market share, by being P&G itself the disruptor, hence increasing the corporation's overall share and securing its possession over a longer period (Govindarajan, 2012).

Regarding brand management, in 1931 Neil McElroy proposed a system in which P&G's "brands would fight with each other for both resources and market share," but didn't give any indications on what to do with the losing brands. In fact, "many corporations generate 80% to 90% of their profits from fewer than 20% of the brands they sell, while they lose money or barely break even on many of the other brands in their portfolios" (Kumar, 2003).

Facing such an ordeal, Jack Welch, while being the CEO of General Electric (1981 to 2001), defined the following strategy: every business had to be either first or second in its sector, or else GE would fix it (transform it), close it, or sell it (divest it) (Roberto, 2011). Coming from the top, such an initiative has to propagate from the strategic level to the operational one, passing by the tactical level. In this sense, the respective level leaders have to improve, eliminate, or outsource those processes, projects, and activities that don't increase the value perceived by the final user of the product or service. Therefore, only the value chain and optimally performed supporting processes, projects, and activities should be kept.

According to Harland et al. (2005), "the most significant reasons for outsourcing are to enable organizations to focus on core activities, to reduce costs, providing short-term financial benefits and balance sheet improvements, [in addition to] 'increased flexibility to configure resources to meet changing market needs.'" In fact, the outsourcing hype led the International Organization for Standardization (ISO) to the creation of Project Committee 259 "in response to the wide range of methodologies that developed at the inception of the outsourcing industry. These had invariably, over time, come to cover similar processes and themes" (Ritchie, 2015). However, the standard defined by this committee (ISO 37500) isn't just a synthesis of methodologies; it also deals with the main causes of outsourcing failures, such as the one stated by Adrian Quayle: "experience has shown that many of the problems arise from the lack of, or poor, governance practices" (as cited in Ritchie, 2015).

At the moment of this writing, outsourcing remains a valid option for altering a company's competitiveness, for better or worse, and ISO 37500 is the new internationally-recognized starting point. However, it alone isn't sufficient to successfully carry on such a venture, as stated in its first paragraph: "This International Standard aims to provide general guidance for outsourcing for any organization in any sector" (ISO, 2014), thus leaving particularities to each company.

I.2. Research Objectives
I.2.1. Main Objective

To propose a toolkit for outsourcing that helps avoid unnecessary adversities, while being compatible with the ISO 37500:2014.

I.2.2. Specific Objectives

- To identify the main issues that hindered recent outsourcing endeavors.
- To determine which methodologies, frameworks, tools, and techniques might help prevent such problems.
- To develop a toolkit for outsourcing that integrates the previously detected methodologies, frameworks, tools, and techniques and is compatible with the ISO 37500:2014.

I.3. Assumptions, Delimitations, and Limitations

Due to time limitations, this research mainly focused on onshore outsourcing initiatives, the ISO 37500:2014, and a set of methodologies, frameworks, tools, and techniques that relate to the author's work experience and fields of knowledge. In particular, seven case studies were related to Information and Communications Technology (ICT) and one to industrial maintenance, which, although being the odd duck, shed light on a series of more tangible, highly relevant outsourcing aspects. Also due to time limitations, the proposed toolkit wasn't tested.

Some other constraints were the author's location, the composition and reach of his social and work networks, and the interviewees' availability. All of these elements highly influenced and conditioned the selection of the sample for the semi-structured interviews and how they were conducted, both matters pertaining to the empirical analysis.

It is assumed that the reader has already glanced through the ISO 37500:2014 and that the company (client) has already determined which are its core and non-core businesses.

I.4. Justification

In conjunction with the ISO 37500, the toolkit proposed by this research will hopefully help companies all over the world avoid, or reduce the impact and likeliness of, the outsourcing risks, extracted from theory and experience, that might otherwise have catastrophically expensive consequences, as exemplified in the Problem Statement and several case studies.

Everyone, from newcomers, enthusiasts, or researchers to outsourcing experts, will expectantly benefit from both the standard and said supplementary toolkit. This shall also hold internationally, as the former document already possesses this characteristic, while the latter will achieve it by including only globally recognized methodologies, frameworks, tools, and techniques, or locally acclaimed but with international applicability.

Last but not least, employees might actually have fun outsourcing, being more confident about it and maybe even establishing more fructiferous relationships, rather than seeing it as a cumbersome endeavor plagued with tedious, ineffective never-ending meetings.

CHAPTER II
REFERENCE FRAMEWORK

Having stated the problem and objectives of this research, it's now possible to proceed with the theoretical foundations upon which the upcoming chapters are built. As such, the Reference Framework contains a set of concepts, theories, methodologies, frameworks, tools, and techniques related, or applicable, to outsourcing.

II.1. Conceptual Framework

This subchapter introduces several concepts that are indispensable for the comprehension of this document, in a sequential and contextualized manner.

II.1.1. Business Process

Back in 1993, Thomas Davenport defined a process as a "structured, measured set of activities designed to produce a specified output for a particular customer or market" and further detailed that it comprises "a specific ordering of work activities across time and place, with a beginning, an end, and clearly identified inputs and outputs" (Davenport, 1993, p. 5).

Building upon this definition, von Scheel et al. described a business process as a "collection of tasks and activities (business operations and actions) consisting of employees, materials, machines, systems, and methods that are being structured in such a way as to design, create, and deliver a product or a service to the consumer" (2014, p. 1).

However, none of these definitions mentioned the events that trigger or initiate a process nor the decision points that may alter a process' execution, which are instead included in Dumas' et aliorum business process definition: "a collection of inter-related events, activities, and decision points that involve a number of actors and objects, which collectively lead to an outcome that is of value to at least one customer" (2018, pp. 3-6). For the scope of this research, the customer may be internal (e.g. another department or functional area) or external (e.g. a client or final consumer) to the company -the same applies to the "consumer" in the previous definition. Dumas et al. illustrated the components of a business process as shown in Figure 1.

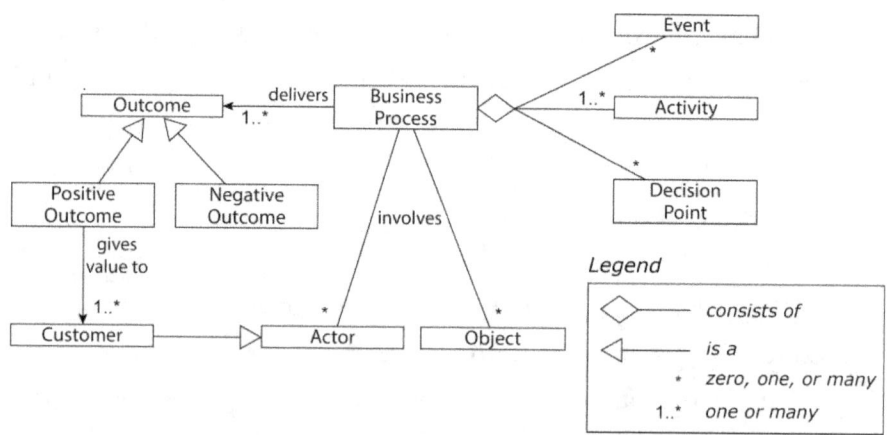

Figure 1. Ingredients of a Business Process

Source: Dumas et al. (2018, p. 6)

II.1.2. Core and Non-Core Business Processes

Harmon (2014, p. 186) distinguishes business processes as: core or operational, management, and enabling or support processes. Yet, he doesn't explicitly provide a definition. Nevertheless, the Business Process Management Common Body of Knowledge (BPM CBoK) (Lee, 2013, p. 60) does:

- Primary/Core/Operational processes are "end-to-end, typically cross-functional processes that directly deliver value to [a] customer" (Lee, 2013, p. 60). Hence, they "must be performed in an exemplary manner to ensure a firm's continued competitiveness" (Core Process, n.d.).
- Enabling/Support processes don't directly deliver such value, but support primary processes in doing so.
- Management processes "measure, monitor, and control business activities. They ensure that primary and support processes are designed and executed in a manner that meets operational, financial, regulatory, and legal goals" (Lee, 2013, p. 60). Although, they don't directly deliver value to customers.

Support and management processes may also be referred to as "non-core."

II.1.3. Sourcing

Another matter to consider is sourcing, which Hinkelman defined as the "location and acquisition of all the vital inputs required for an organization to operate [including] raw materials, component parts, products, labor in all its forms, location and services" (2008, p. 578). He also listed three components that were held crucial to successful sourcing:

- The acquisition of products and services of sufficient quality,
- The securing of an uninterrupted supply of products and services, and
- The acquisition of products and services at the most competitive prices possible (Hinkelman, 2008, p. 580).

Although this sourcing approach was followed for several decades, another method was proposed.

II.1.3.1. Sourcing Strategy and Strategic Sourcing

Specifically, the ISO 37500 defined a sourcing strategy as an "organization's action plan to obtain products and services that are essential to run its business in the most effective and efficient manner" (2014, p. 4). Similarly, Parniangtong described strategic sourcing as "the process of developing channels of supply at the *lowest total cost*, not just the lowest purchase price" (2016, p. 5), hence reconsidering Hinkelman's last component. In fact, Parniangtong indicated three "fundamental philosophies":

- Focus on the total delivered value, not the purchase price;
- Collaborative approach to dealing with suppliers, rather than oversight; and
- Focus on enhancing profitability, rather than cost savings.

Evidently, this approach is different, as it's more interested in maximizing value, rather than merely negotiating for the lowest prices, and regards sourcing as a longer-term venture, establishing cooperative relationships with providers.

Additionally, a sourcing strategy specifies "how many suppliers a firm will have for one specific component/product/service, given the importance of the component and the structure of the supply market, and how the suppliers are related to each other" (Najafi, Holmen, Lind, & Pedersen, 2014, p. 2). The most common sourcing structures are single sourcing, in which a specific product or service is purchased from a single supplier, and multi-sourcing, in which it's purchased from multiple suppliers.

II.1.3.2. Outsourcing

A company may decide to outsource or "obtain (goods or a service) from an outside or foreign supplier, especially in place of an internal source[, or to] contract (work) out or abroad" (Outsource, n.d.). Two elements pop up from this definition: the location of the supplier and the replacement of an internal source. The former is discussed in Section II.1.3.4.

As of the latter, Gilley and Rasheed (2000, pp. 764-765) indicate that outsourcing may regard two matters: the *substitution* of internal activities with external purchases (i.e. vertical disintegration) or the *abstention* from completing goods or services in-house, although being capable of doing so, and purchasing them externally (i.e. make or buy).

Meanwhile, Hinkelman provides insight on the kinds of activities to be performed by the counterpart, when he defines outsourcing as the "contracting of the management and/or execution of a business function to an outside third-party contractor or subcontractor" (2008, p. 580).

Finally, the ISO 37500 considers outsourcing to be a "business model for the delivery of a product or services to a client by a provider"

(ISO, 2014, p. 3).

II.1.3.3. Parties

There are two main parties involved in this type of endeavor: the client and the provider, although they may be called differently. The client may be referred to as the outsourcer, buyer, or contractor. While the provider may be regarded as the outsourcee, vendor, contractee, or supplier.

Although there certainly are subtleties among each of these concepts, for the purposes of this research, they're considered synonyms within their groups and are used interchangeably.

With respect to their meanings, the ISO 37500 defines a client as an "individual or group of organizations entering into an agreement with a provider for products and services for their own use" (ISO, 2014, p. 2) and a provider as an "organization that offers a product or service to a client" (p. 3).

II.1.3.4. Provider's Location

Although outsourcing was previously discussed, other kinds of sourcing relationships are possible, depending on the provider's location with respect to the client.

While in *out*sourcing or *dis*integration (vertical or lateral) the provider is a non-client entity (located outside of the client's domain), in *in*sourcing or integration (vertical or lateral) the provider lies within the client's domain. Thus, if the relationship were established between two different companies or corporate groups, it would be considered outsourcing. However, if it were established between two subsidiaries or companies of the same corporate group, or two departments of the same company, it would be regarded as insourcing.

Another term is *back*sourcing or *re*integration (vertical or lateral), which denotes the reversal of an outsourcing relationship, returning to insourcing. For example, a client that performed (insourced), or could've performed, a particular process internally eventually decided to outsource it to an external provider. However, later on, the client chose to return to performing said process internally, backsourcing it.

Similarly, *home*sourcing or *home*shoring refers to the "transfer of employment from company offices to employees' homes" (Homeshoring, n.d.) or to those of independent contractors, as a combination of outsourcing and telecommuting (Hinkelman, 2008, p. 582).

Up to now, the terms related to the inter-/intra-organizational location of the provider with respect to the client (out-, in-, back-, and homesourcing) have been defined. However, there's another set of concepts that focus on the physical location of the provider with respect to the client.

In particular, an *off*shore provider is located in a country far away from that in which the client is based. Instead, if the countries were nearby, even sharing a border, the provider would be *near*shore (Sourcingmag.com, n.d.). The Economist defines it as the "business of moving production, research and business processes to countries that are quite cheap and very close rather than very cheap and far away" (2005). In both of these cases, the provider may also be described as *global*. Oppositely, an *in*shore, *on*shore, or domestic provider is located in the same country as the client.

Finally, *re*shoring or *back*shoring a provider "is the process of returning the production and manufacturing of goods [or the performance of services] back to the [client's] original country" (Reshoring, n.d.).

Even though this research mainly focuses on outsourcing, the aforementioned concepts should help the reader gain a better understanding of the sourcing context, as summarized in Table 1 and Figure 2.

Table 1. Types of Sourcing Relationships

Type of sourcing	Provider's Physical Location[a]	Provider's Organizational Location[a]
Onshore **in**sourcing	Same country	Same company/corporate group
Offshore **in**sourcing	Different country	Same company/corporate group
Onshore **out**sourcing	Same country	Different company
Offshore **out**sourcing	Different country	Different company
Homesourcing	Any country (home)	Same or different company

[a]: with respect to the client

Source: Prepared by the author

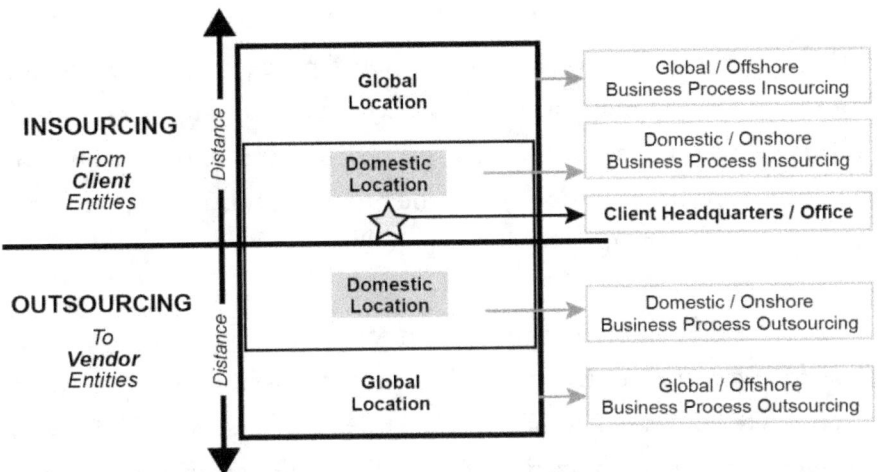

Figure 2. Types of Sourcing Relationships
Source: Chakrabarty (2007, p. 210)

II.1.4. Sub-Outsourcing

Sub-outsourcing, also denominated subcontracting or chain-outsourcing, refers to "a situation where the service provider under an outsourcing arrangement further transfers a process, a service or an activity, or parts thereof, to another service provider" (EBA European Banking Authority, 2018, p. 19). For example, a client outsources a specific service to a provider, who in turn has another provider perform some of the activities necessary for said service.

Since some countries impose a limit on the percentage of the total activities that may be chain-outsourced, the reader should check the local legislation on this matter.

II.1.5. Business Process Outsourcing

By combining the concepts of business process and outsourcing, Rouse (2018) defines business process outsourcing (BPO) as a "business practice in which one organization hires another company to perform a task (i.e. process) that the hiring organization requires for its own business to successfully operate."

In particular, an organization might choose to outsource an entire department or functional area, or a specific business process, which could cover activities of a single department or of several, thus being transversal to the organization. As of the business functions, they're usually divided into two categories: back-office and front-office. Normally, the latter interacts with the customer, while the former doesn't. Some examples of the former are: accounting, human resources (HR), information technology (IT) services, payment processing, purchasing, regulatory compliance, and quality assurance (QA). On the other end, front-office processes include customer-related services like marketing, sales, trading, and technical support.

II.2. Theoretical Framework

This subchapter presents eight case studies (summarized in Section II.2.1.9), then proceeds with the methodologies, frameworks, tools, and techniques that were suggested by interviewees (see Chapter IV), the author, or other literature, as a means to avoid the unnecessary adversities extracted from said cases and interviews.

II.2.1. Case Studies

This section begins with three Anglo-Saxon outsourcing failures, then presents the setbacks of a Kuwaiti public-sector organization, moves on to two Polish SME cases, and closes with two unsuccessful ventures that led to backsourcing in Brazil and France. In most cases, the researchers assigned codenames to the companies, for anonymity purposes.

II.2.1.1. Case 1: Queensland's Health Department and IBM

In the first Anglo-Saxon case, IBM won a contract with Queensland's Health Department to develop a payroll administration software, which "was originally supposed to cost AUS$6 million and escalated into an out-of-control AUS$1.2 billion" (Bort, 2013). The inquiry "tied a number of IBM employees working on the contract bid to serious ethical transgressions, including using leaked information about competitors to gain advantage and attempting to access tender responses by opposing bidders Logica and Accenture" (Cowan, 2016).

However, in addition to improperly vetting the providers, the client "was passive, perhaps lazy, in the identification and communication of its business requirements, with the result that it did not communicate to IBM all the requirements necessary to produce a functional (albeit minimal and interim) payroll system" (Chesterman, 2013, p. 94). Consequently, during this period thousands of client employees didn't get their paychecks while others were overpaid. Under these circumstances, the client ended up paying 200 times the initial price for a product that took years to develop and still didn't satisfy its needs (Garland, 2015).

II.2.1.2. Case 2: U.S. Navy and Marine Corps and Electronic Data Systems

With respect to the second Anglo-Saxon case, Electronic Data Systems (EDS) won the largest computer outsourcing contract ever awarded, with the goal of making

> The naval service more efficient, more productive and
> enhance its readiness by providing video and voice
> communications to link shore units and interface with the
> "Information Technology for the 21st Century" (IT-21)
> initiative and the Marine Corps Tactical Network
> (MCTN)...[, via] a single hacker-proof network that
> would link 345,000 computers at 4000 Navy and Marine
> location[s] domestically and internationally (Intranet
> Development Project, n.d.).

Yet, EDS' failure to appropriately foresee and delimit the project's
scope (Garland, 2015) caused it a loss of $375 million (Oates, 2004).

II.2.1.3. Case 3: Virgin Airlines and Navitaire

As of the third Anglo-Saxon case, Virgin Airlines was grounded by
the FAA because its cloud-based IT provider, Navitaire, had a hard
drive failure that took almost 24 hours to fix, which led to "more than
50,000 passengers [being left] stranded and frustrated" (Garland, 2015)
and $15 million to $20 million of losses for the client (LeMay, 2010).

II.2.1.4. Case 4: Alpha and Omega

Next, Khalfan (2003) examined a BPO project in Kuwait, between
a large public-sector organization (Alpha; client) and an internationally
prestigious software consulting firm (Omega; provider), that resulted
in a complete failure and cost several millions. More specifically, the
main purpose of this project was to computerize Alpha by producing
a custom-built software solution, to support the organization's
processes and replace an obsolete system. After a few meetings with

Omega, aimed at obtaining its opinions and suggestions about the initiative, the client negotiated a deal and directly awarded the contract to this provider.

Not much time later, obstacles and delays began to appear when the consultants tried to determine Alpha's business requirements, due to the "high variability and uncertainty of business processes" (p. 752), and proposed the re-engineering of many such processes. Unexpectedly, the client's top management rejected several of these changes, for which Khalfan conjectured a series of reasons, including political issues and the impending elimination of jobs, as a consequence of the more efficient processes. So, the lack of commitment and involvement of the client's top management in the project clearly manifested itself upon the end-users, who didn't cooperate much.

Additionally, the provider's team was composed of consultants from different countries. This generated a cultural gap with the client's personnel that took time and effort to compensate. In fact, after three years no real progress had been made and Omega's initial team had changed twice due to Alpha's request, for which it didn't offer "justifiable reasons" (p. 754). At this point, Omega decided to withdraw from the contract, stating its inability to develop the system.

II.2.1.5. Case 5: SVX-1 and SoftGal

Moving on, in 2015 Prystupa and Rządca analyzed a couple of failed Polish SME outsourcing ventures.

The first case (SVX-1) consisted of an unplanned transition in the family business, accompanied by a hasty, naïve outsourcing initiative that unfortunately, although predictably, drove the company to bankruptcy. It all began when the owner died, leaving an SME dedicated to antivirus software development and seven heirs, of whom only two were adults (the oldest son and the owner's step-wife). Successively, the 21-year-old son had to take control of the company. As the former president left and started his own business in the same sector, hence becoming a direct competitor, the son hired an experienced managing director. However, the situation further worsened as 15 development team members chose to work for the former president's company.

At this point, the son and managing director decided to outsource a development team, expecting qualified professionals. Yet, the hastily signed contract, without appropriately vetting the provider (SoftGal), led to a commitment with a company that didn't have experts in the antivirus field and that mainly focused on the appearance of the software, setting aside the product's core functionalities (i.e. virus detection and neutralization or elimination). Additionally, since no clause regarding penalties (malus) for the deliverables' lack of quality was stipulated, customers complained.

Even though the client tried to backsource as a last resort, the reputational damage had already set the company on the path towards bankruptcy.

II.2.1.6. Case 6: GFT-1 and Flemings

With respect to the second Polish case, two young entrepreneurs created a computer game development business (GFT-1). After two failed attempts, the third game turned out to be a success and they sold the property rights to a famous publisher. Next, they invested this money in the development of a new game. Although, in order to avoid going negative, they decided to work on a second game, simultaneously. However, due to the limited amount of human resources available and the rapidly changing market, they chose to outsource the development of one of these games to a notable local studio: Flemings.

Everything seemed to be going well, but this perception changed when the client received the first version of the game. It didn't satisfy the quality expectations and, even though the two entrepreneurs could've terminated the contract, they didn't do so at the time. A few months later, they did. So, the provider finished the technical aspects, whereas the design was completed internally. Regrettably, the final product didn't make ends meet at the marketplace (Prystupa & Rządca, 2015).

II.2.1.7. Case 7: Organization X

The next case (Cabral, Quelin, & Maia, 2014) is about a large metallurgical company (code-named Organization X) in Brazil that opted to outsource the industrial maintenance services and later on reverted such decision. Although this case is more related to operational services than all the others, it was included because it offers a more tangible scenario containing certain aspects that are deemed relevant for any kind of outsourcing operation: bandwagon behavior, employee exodus, occupational hazards, contract duration, and eventual backsourcing.

The main reasons for outsourcing were cost reduction, competitiveness increase, and mimesis or bandwagon behavior (i.e. because "everybody was outsourcing"), in addition to industrial maintenance not being considered a core function. Throughout the endeavor, which was meant to last up to two years, the client kept some employees to supervise the providers. Nevertheless, the expected savings were never achieved.

Although the providers rose their prices, they increased their employees' wages only by a fraction, so many left, including the most experienced. Unfortunately, the remaining outsourced employees were three times more propense to occupational hazards, due to their "lower qualifications … and … lack of commitment to internal work safety procedures" (p. 369). Evidently, the quality of the services offered by the providers decreased. Simultaneously, some judges ruled that the client should offer the same benefits to the providers' personnel as it did to its own.

Also, the contract's duration seems to have influenced the outcome, since "the presence of uncertainty regarding contract renewal and the short time to cover the investment in specific human assets gave rise to underinvestment on the contractor's side in skilled labor" (p. 370).

Eventually, Organization X decided to backsource these services, but the examination of such a reversal operation is left to the reader, as it goes beyond the scope of this research. Nonetheless, Table 2 might help illustrate the case.

Table 2. Outsourcing vs. Backsourcing at Organization X

Outsourced personnel	Backsourced personnel
Low qualified personnel.	Assurance of manpower's qualification by using the recruiting procedures of Organization X.
Low levels of motivation and commitment.	There are more possibilities to motivate employees.
Contractual terms (every two years) generate discontinuities in the process.	Probability of discontinuities in the process is lower.
Total costs include labor costs and contractor's profit.	Cost savings due to elimination of the contractor's profit.
Require the assignment of contract supervisors.	Contract supervisors are not needed. Personnel can be reallocated to maintenance activities.
Increased odds of suffering labor accidents.	Labor accident risks decrease.
Overestimation of the work force needs.	Fewer personnel needed.
More chances of having judicial disputes in labor courts.	Judicial dispute odds are lower.

Source: Adapted from Cabral, Quelin, & Maia (2014, p. 370)

II.2.1.8. Case 8: Teleco and Prov-A

The last case study presented in this research was written by Florence Law (2018), who examined a situation similar to the one in the previous case, in the sense that it regards a client that outsourced a set of services, but after several years decided to backsource them. Law codenamed the client, a French telecommunications operator, Teleco and the provider Prov-A.

During the first phase "Outsourcing lock-in" and for more than ten years, Teleco used an IT governance structure that allowed IT managers to choose among "hiring IT staff, contracting with independent consultants, or signing fixed contracts with outsourcing firms" (p. 345). As the growth rate of this market sector diminished in France, Teleco tightened the lease, hence reducing the use of consultants and setting hiring caps for periods of three years. By the tenth year since the beginning of this phase, 38% of its IT human resources was composed by internal employees, while the remaining 62%, by external resources. The former mainly comprised project managers who monitored the outsourced projects. In fact, "the firm developed strong capabilities in designing, monitoring, and ensuring outsourcing contracts with frequent and regular meetings with outsourcers and the use by outsourcers of Teleco's specific IT project management methods" (p. 346), so from this point of view the company seemed bulletproof.

Nevertheless, a crisis emerged and with it, the second phase: "Organizational crisis." Prov-A couldn't keep up with the development of frequent updates for Teleco's Alpha system, which interfaced with its partners' systems. These updates helped Teleco stay competitive and adapt to market demand. Tactlessly, yet opportunistically, the provider didn't assign the right people to this service, i.e. they lacked the required qualifications. Therefore, Alpha failed and this resulted in the decay of the client's reputation and the stakeholders lost their trust in Teleco's management.

At this point, the third phase began: "Emergency backsourcing." Since the client needed to solve the problem fast, searching for other providers to replace Prov-A wasn't a feasible solution, as it would've taken months and a better performance wasn't guaranteed. So, Teleco decided to backsource.

Although, as stated in the previous case, backsourcing lies beyond the scope of this research, knowing one particular detail might result helpful when preparing for an outsourcing venture. Namely, even though Teleco's workforce had diminished with outsourcing, it managed to keep a certain amount of internal of employees that, possessing the required knowledge and skills, was able to quickly take control of the Alpha situation.

II.2.1.9. Summary

To sum up the analysis of these cases, taking into account this research's first specific objective, Table 3 exhibits their main characteristics.

Table 3. Case Study Summary

Case	Field	Adversities and Results	Causes
1	Software development	• Thousands of employees didn't get their paychecks while others were overpaid • The client paid 200 times the initial price • The product took years to develop • The product didn't satisfy the client's needs	• The client improperly vetted the provider • The client was passive in the identification of its business requirements
2	Communications technology	• The provider lost $375 million	• The provider failed to appropriately foresee and delimit the project's scope
3	Cloud-based IT systems	• More than 50,000 passengers were left stranded • The client lost $15-20 million	• Both the client and provider failed to properly assess the risk of a hard drive failure and manage it accordingly
4	Software development	• The provider was asked to replace its team members twice • After three years, no real progress was made	• The client directly awarded the contract without inviting other providers to a vendor selection process

		• The provider withdrew from the contract	• High variability and uncertainty of business processes • Political and cultural issues • Lack of commitment from the client's personnel
5	Software development	• The provider didn't have experts in antivirus development • The customers complained about the antivirus' lack of quality • The client tried backsourcing, but couldn't recover from the reputational damage • The client went bankrupt	• Unplanned transition in the family business • Client's employee exodus, including the former president • Outsourcing undertaken naïvely and hastily, without appropriately vetting the vendor nor stipulating a malus clause for quality • The client outsourced its core business • No monitoring and control mechanisms were established
6	Game development	• The provider's first deliverable didn't meet the expectations • The client tried backsourcing, but the final product didn't meet market needs	• Outsourcing undertaken without appropriately vetting the vendor • The client outsourced core activities to compensate for lack of personnel • No adequate monitoring and control mechanisms were established
7	Industrial maintenance	• Providers' remaining employees were more	• Outsourcing possibly undertaken for bandwagon behavior

		propense to occupational hazards • Lawsuits: judges determined that the client should offer the same benefits of its employees to the vendors' personnel • The quality of the providers' services decreased • The provider didn't invest much due to the short contract renewal period • The client's expected savings weren't achieved • The client decided to back-source	• Industrial maintenance was considered a non-core function • Providers' employee exodus, including the most qualified • Disparity between the benefits received by the client's and providers' employees • Unmotivated outsourced personnel • Contract renewal every two years
8	Software update development	• The provider couldn't keep up with the client's frequent update requirements • The system failed • The client's reputation decayed • Stakeholders lost their trust in the client's management • The client decided to backsource and was successful, thanks to its IT governance structure	• Market sector's growth diminished • The client mainly kept project managers who monitored the outsourced projects • The provider didn't assign the right people to the service

Source: Prepared by the author

At this point, it might be safe to repeat the phrase: "The causes of most major failed outsourcing projects go back to before they were outsourced" (Most outsourcing failures flawed before they start, 2004).

II.2.2. Methodologies, Frameworks, Tools, and Techniques

Moving on, this section presents the methodologies, frameworks, tools, and techniques that were used to build the toolkit (Chapter V), with the purpose of avoiding the unnecessary adversities revealed by the case studies and interviews (see Section III.2.3 and Chapter IV, respectively), through the addressment of their main causes. Starting with a short description of the ISO 37500:2014, UML use case diagrams, flowcharts, BPMN diagrams, proceeding with the PMBoK Guide, ITIL, Six Sigma, and concluding with effective meeting considerations.

II.2.2.1. ISO 37500:2014

In 2014, the International Organization for Standardization published its first standard on outsourcing, i.e. ISO 37500. This document "aims to provide general guidance for outsourcing for any organization in any sector" (ISO, 2014, p. vi). In other words, it's meant to be tailored to company-specific, or industry-specific, needs. In fact, before applying the proposed model, the client should've "established a sourcing strategy and concluded that outsourcing might be a beneficial approach" (p. vi).

The main feature of this standard is its life cycle model, which consists of four phases, as illustrated in Figure 3:

1. Outsourcing strategy analysis (both sourcing and exit strategies),

2. Initiation and selection (of the provider),

3. Transition (into outsourcing), and

4. Deliver value.

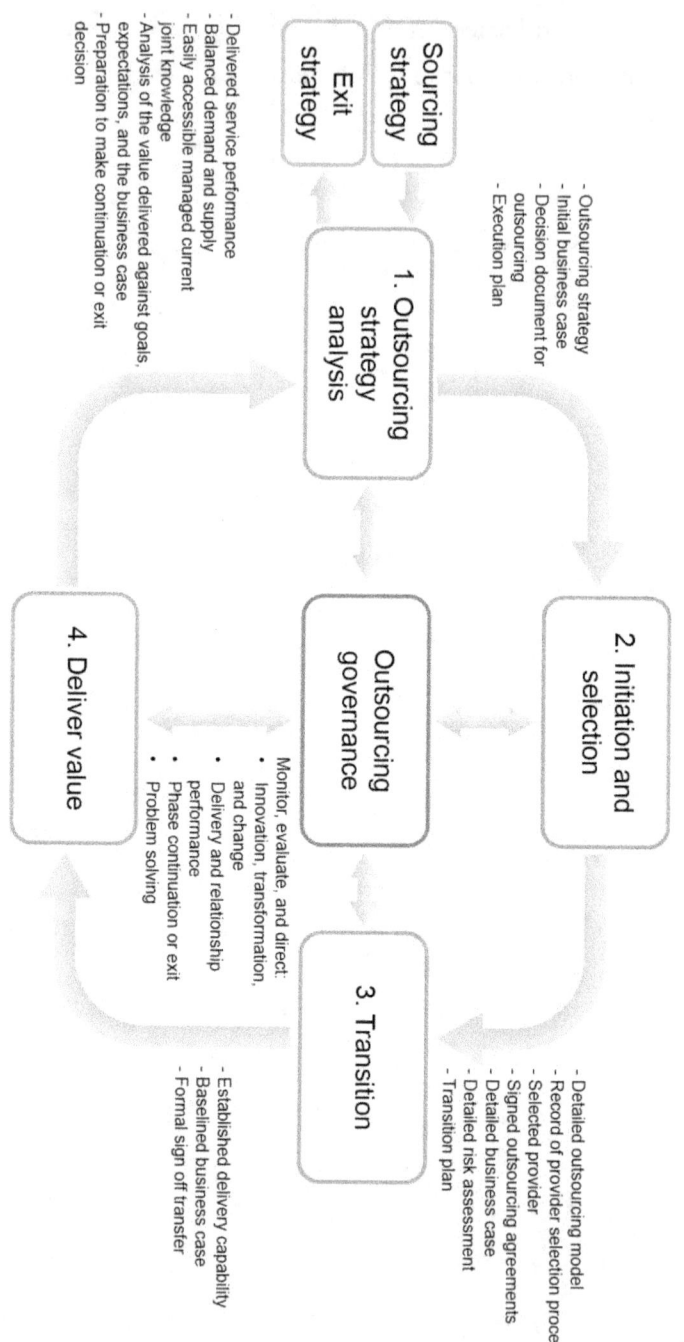

Figure 3. Main Outputs of the Outsourcing Life Cycle Model
Source: ISO 37500:2014 (p. 9)

Each of these phases, in turn, contains a set of processes regarding its purpose, main activities to be performed, key success factors, and main inputs and outputs (which were included as side notes in Figure 3).

Although some managers may believe that outsourcing helps lighten their workload, it "requires more, not less governance. You cannot outsource to a third party your responsibility for getting the job done" (Stern, 2007). In fact, as the reader might've noticed in Figure 3, the standard advises the creation of an outsourcing governance function and places it at the center of its life cycle model, to continuously monitor, evaluate, and direct each of the four phases, while favoring collaboration among parties, facilitating effective decision making by the joint leadership, appreciating cultural differences, ensuring the pursuit of the desired strategic results, and mitigating risks.

The purpose of the first phase (Outsourcing strategy analysis) is to discover and evaluate outsourcing opportunities, and to define and sustain an outsourcing strategy that meets business goals and requirements, comprehensive of a preliminary business case.

During the second phase (Initiation and selection), the client-to-be shall specify a list of requirements for the services to be outsourced, which will then be published or sent to exclusive providers, who might in turn respond with a proposal. Afterwards, the providers deemed appropriate will be selected and the outsourcing agreements, successfully formalized. However, if the updated business case were considered too risky or with a high degree of uncertainty, the life cycle could be restarted, returning to the first phase.

Subsequently, the third phase (Transition) englobes the eventual transfer of staff, assets, and related change management procedures. Once the provider's capability to fulfil the previously agreed requirements is confirmed, taking into account its quality and performance levels, the outsourced services and respective responsibility can be officially handed over. Although, if the outsourcing venture turned out to be more expensive than expected or the updated business case were no longer retained feasible, the abandonment of the outsourcing process should be considered, hence returning to the first phase.

Finally, the fourth and last phase (Deliver value) is dedicated to making sure that both parties realize and sustain the benefits of the outsourcing agreement. The provider focuses on appropriately satisfying the stipulated requirements, while the client, on monitoring its service provision.

Then, the cycle recommences.

Throughout the life cycle, the following outsourcing risks (pp. 5-6) should be considered to increase the probability of success, (in addition to a list of potential risks (p. 56), which the reader is strongly advised to review):

- Absence of a strategy;
- Poor understanding of environment dynamics, emphasizing the importance of outsourcing governance;
- Blind focus on cost reduction, picking up on the strategic sourcing discussion (see II.1.3.1) and adding the impact and risks of outsourcing;
- Underestimated business impact, requiring a clear, visible, and committed strategic leadership to guide the organizational

change;

- Poor cultural compatibility;
- Poor understanding of the process by the client; and
- Poor relationship management.

So, although this was a brief overview of the ISO 37500:2014, it should transmit the importance, relevance, and usefulness of this standard, especially when considering the previous case studies (see Table 3).

II.2.2.2. UML Use Case Diagrams

Unified Modeling Language (UML) use case diagrams could support outsourcing endeavors, for example by identifying the activities a certain role can perform. It is mainly composed of symbols, each of which is interpreted in a specific manner.

Symbol	Reference Name
 (actor stick figure symbol)	Actor
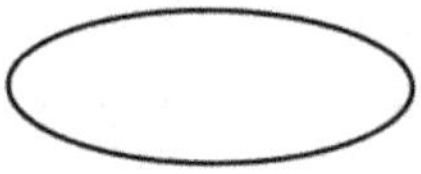 (ellipse symbol)	Use case
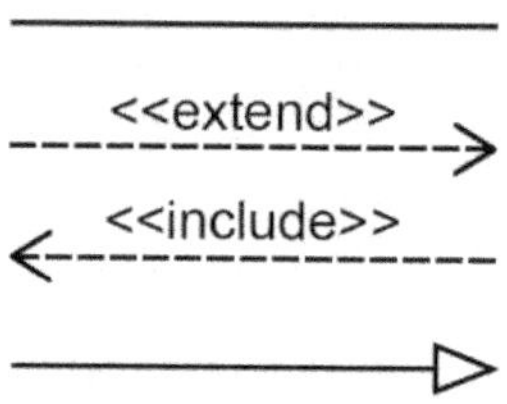 <<extend>> ----------> <----------<<include>> ————————▷	Relationship

Figure 4. UML Use Case Diagram Symbols
Source: Vu (2015, p. 82)

   The actor symbol is normally used to represent a role, system, or a particular person. A use case is an action that the actor can perform and the relationship connectors indicate how use cases relate to each other. Additionally, these diagrams are usually accompanied by a document describing each use case, providing further details about the actors, priorities, pre-conditions, post-conditions, flows of events, and scenarios, among other information (Schneider & Winters, 2001, pp. 113-115).

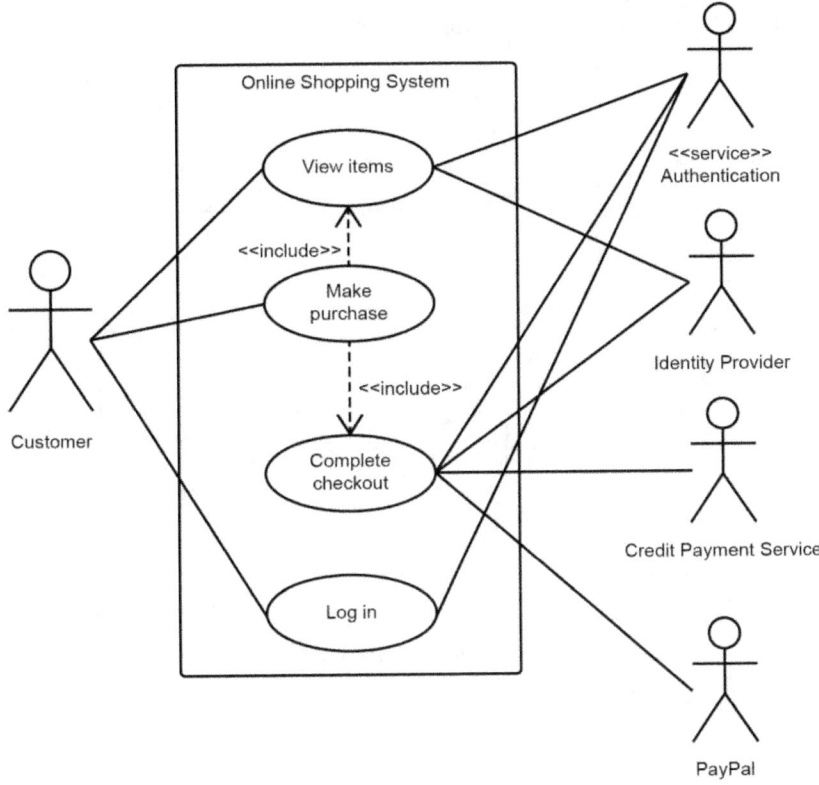

Figure 5. UML Use Case Diagram Example
Source: Lucid Software Inc. (UML Use Case Diagram Tutorial, n.d.)

It shall be noted that this kind of diagram isn't meant to depict a sequence of activities, just what an actor can do in a certain context.

II.2.2.3. Flowcharts

Another standard, distinctively the ISO/IEC 2382:2015, provides a common set of definitions for Information Technology terms. Specifically, it describes a flowchart as the "graphical representation of a process or step-by-step solution of a problem, using suitably annotated geometric figures connected by flowlines for the purpose of designing or documenting a process or program" (ISO/IEC, 2015).

To illustrate this definition, the Software and Systems Engineering Vocabulary website offers the following diagram as an example:

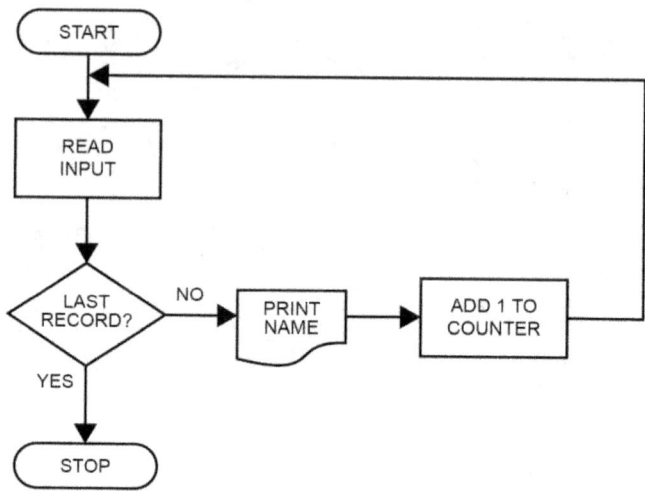

Figure 6. Flowchart Example

Source: (flowchart, n.d.)

Although flowcharts are heavily used in algorithm design, as the one shown in the example, it has also been applied to process design or representation. Evidently, each symbol has its own meaning and Feldmann et al. shared a subset of those included in the ISO 5807:1985, while using them to outline a series of processes followed in a research about tsetse flies:

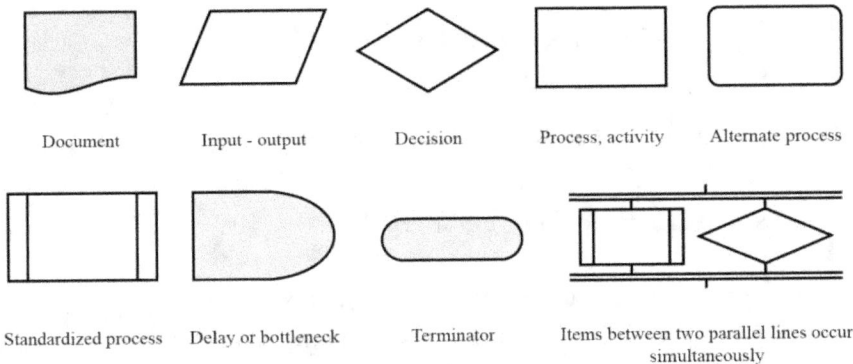

Figure 7. Flowchart Symbols

Source: Feldmann et al. (2018)

However, if the purpose of the diagram were to represent several actors or systems interacting with each other, flowcharts wouldn't be the ideal choice.

II.2.2.4. Business Process Modeling Notation

Instead, the use of Business Process Modeling Notation (BPMN) diagrams is advised. Although it's more comprehensive than the previous couple of representation tools and techniques, its complexity makes it more time-consuming. So, recollecting Dumas' et aliorum definition of a business process (Section II.1.1) and its components and participants (i.e. event, activity, decision point, actor, object, outcome, customer), BPMN diagrams were created and have been optimized to represent all these features, in the most efficient and effective manner.

According to the BPMN, said components and participants are grouped into:

- Flow objects: events, activities, gateways;

- Connecting objects: sequence flow, message flow, association;
- Swimlanes: pool or lane;
- Artifacts: data object, group, annotation;

And some are depicted in Figure 8.

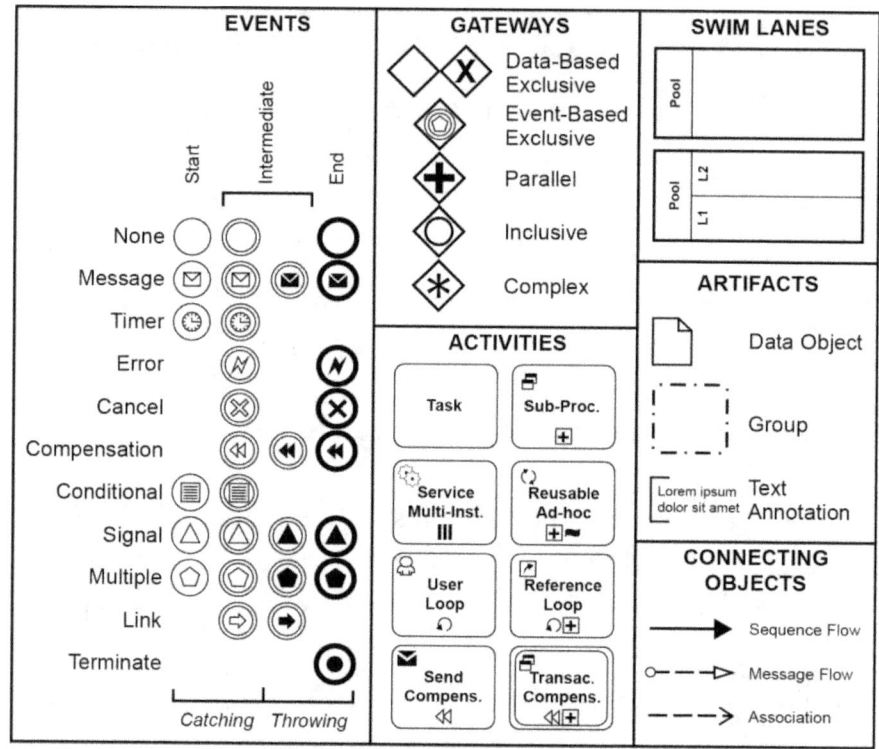

Figure 8. BPMN Elements

Source: Suchenia & Ligęza (2015, p. 790)

Here, the flow objects (events, gateways, and activities) were placed in the first two columns and the rest, in the third. Of these, the pools, lanes, and gateways might be the least intuitive. The Lucid Software Inc. (What is Business Process Modeling Notation, n.d.) indicates that:

A pool represents major participants in a process. A different pool may be in a different company or department but still involved in the process. Swimlanes within a pool show the activities and flow for a certain role or participant, defining who is accountable for what parts of the process.

Meanwhile, it defined a gateway as a "decision point that can adjust the path based on conditions or events [and] be exclusive or inclusive, parallel, complex, or based on data or events."

For example, the BPMN diagram of Figure 9 illustrates an order-to-cash (O2C or OTC) business process for a Chinese restaurant:

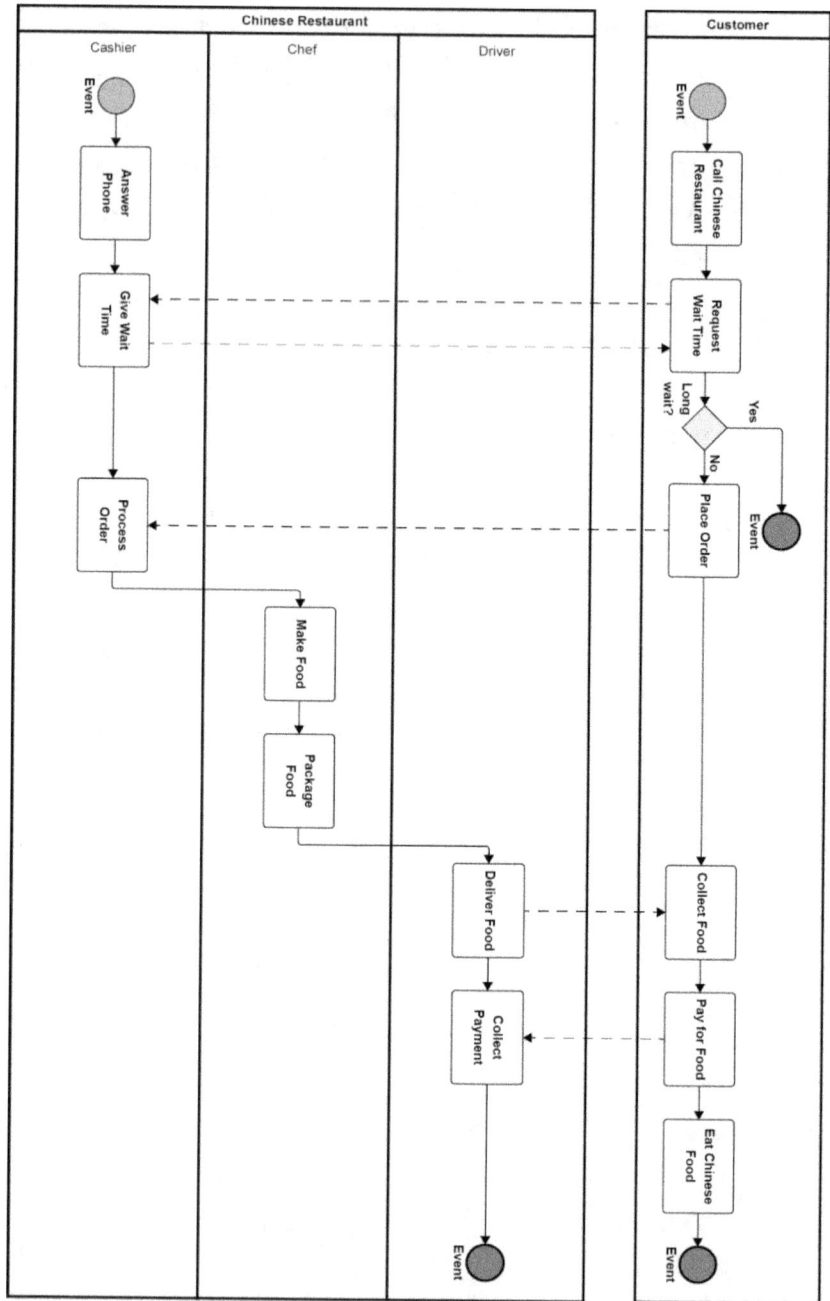

Figure 9. BPMN Diagram Example

Source: Lucid Software Inc. (Diagrams for Dummies: A BPMN Tutorial, n.d.)

By allowing the customer to be both internal and external to the company, this kind of diagram could be used to represent most processes.

II.2.2.5. PMBoK Guide

The Project Management Body of Knowledge (PMBoK) Guide was created by the Project Management Institute (PMI) as a "foundation upon which organizations can build methodologies, policies, procedures, rules, tools and techniques, and life cycle phases needed to practice project management" (Project Management Institute, 2017, p. 2). Its structure is similar to that of the ISO 37500, in the sense that, after presenting a general overview, it delves into each of its project management processes, identifying the inputs and outputs, in addition to relevant tools and techniques.

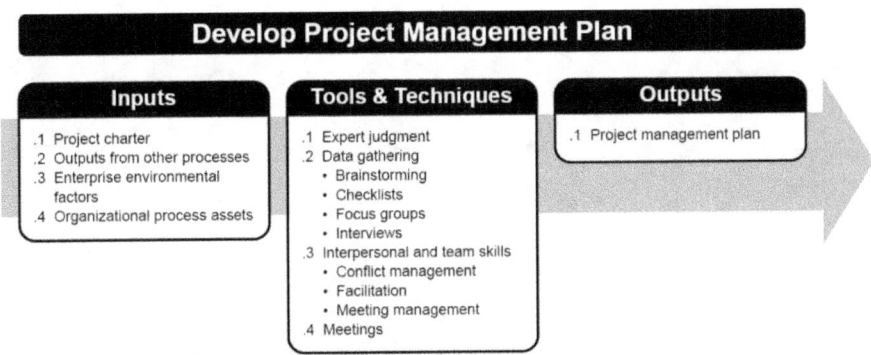

Figure 10. Develop Project Management Plan
Source: Project Management Institute (2017, p. 82)

PMI organized these processes into groups, according to the project phase (i.e. initiation, planning, execution, monitoring and controlling, and closure), and associated them with a specific knowledge area (i.e. integration, scope, schedule, cost, quality, resource, communications, risk, procurement, and stakeholder management). Then, summed them up in the process group and knowledge area map (Figure 11).

Knowledge Areas	Project Management Process Groups				
	Initiating Process Group	Planning Process Group	Executing Process Group	Monitoring and Controlling Process Group	Closing Process Group
4. Project Integration Management	4.1 Develop Project Charter	4.2 Develop Project Management Plan	4.3 Direct and Manage Project Work 4.4 Manage Project Knowledge	4.5 Monitor and Control Project Work 4.6 Perform Integrated Change Control	4.7 Close Project or Phase
5. Project Scope Management		5.1 Plan Scope Management 5.2 Collect Requirements 5.3 Define Scope 5.4 Create WBS		5.5 Validate Scope 5.6 Control Scope	
6. Project Schedule Management		6.1 Plan Schedule Management 6.2 Define Activities 6.3 Sequence Activities 6.4 Estimate Activity Durations 6.5 Develop Schedule		6.6 Control Schedule	
7. Project Cost Management		7.1 Plan Cost Management 7.2 Estimate Costs 7.3 Determine Budget		7.4 Control Costs	
8. Project Quality Management		8.1 Plan Quality Management	8.2 Manage Quality	8.3 Control Quality	
9. Project Resource Management		9.1 Plan Resource Management 9.2 Estimate Activity Resources	9.3 Acquire Resources 9.4 Develop Team 9.5 Manage Team	9.6 Control Resources	
10. Project Communications Management		10.1 Plan Communications Management	10.2 Manage Communications	10.3 Monitor Communications	
11. Project Risk Management		11.1 Plan Risk Management 11.2 Identify Risks 11.3 Perform Qualitative Risk Analysis 11.4 Perform Quantitative Risk Analysis 11.5 Plan Risk Responses	11.6 Implement Risk Responses	11.7 Monitor Risks	
12. Project Procurement Management		12.1 Plan Procurement Management	12.2 Conduct Procurements	12.3 Control Procurements	
13. Project Stakeholder Management	13.1 Identify Stakeholders	13.2 Plan Stakeholder Engagement	13.3 Manage Stakeholder Engagement	13.4 Monitor Stakeholder Engagement	

Figure 11. Project Management Process Group and Knowledge Area Mapping

Source: Project Management Institute (2017, p. 25)

II.2.2.6. ITIL

Instead, the Information Technology Infrastructure Library (ITIL) has been adopted mainly for IT services and is a widely recognized best practice in the IT industry. Its first version was published in 1989 by the Central Computing and Telecommunications Agency (CCTA), a British government agency, and is now a part of the repertoire of AXELOS Ltd.

Being a descriptive, rather than prescriptive, framework, it provides technology-independent guidelines that may be adopted by many different kinds of organizations for IT-related services.

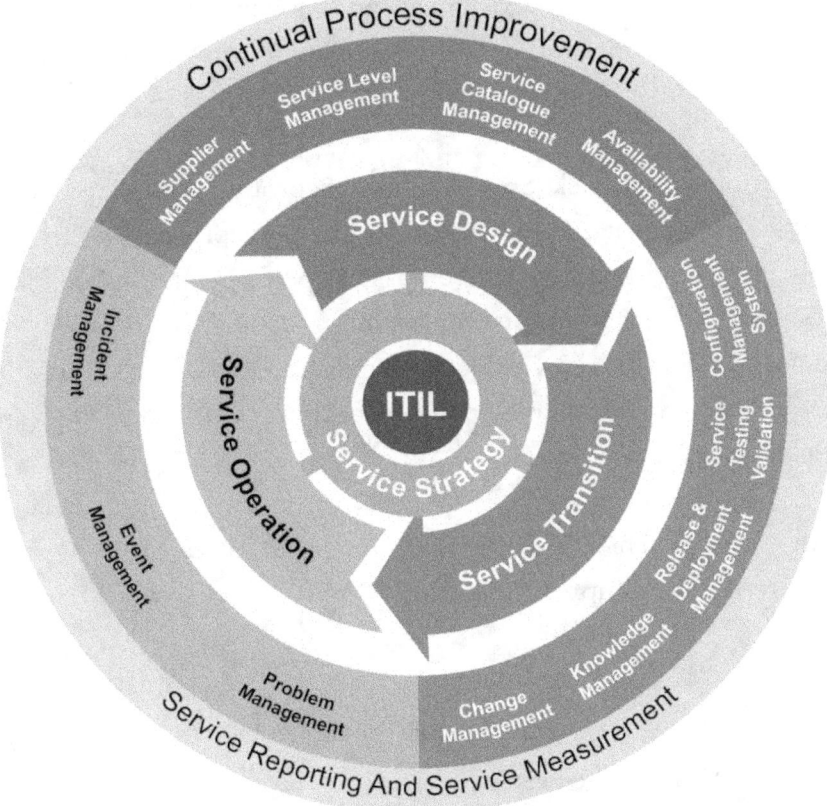

Figure 12. ITIL Service Lifecycle Diagram
Source: SlideModel (n.d.)

As illustrated in Figure 12, ITIL consists of five stages, listed from the center outwards: Service Strategy, Service Design, Service Transition, Service Operation, and Continual Service/Process Improvement.

II.2.2.7. Six Sigma

While the PMBoK Guide and ITIL are purely oriented towards projects and services, respectively, both in some way deal with quality assurance and control techniques. However, Six Sigma focuses on quality and process improvement and is applicable to multiple industries. On top of that, its combination with either tool will probably lead to a greater success rate.

According to Pyzdek, Six Sigma is a "rigorous, focused and highly effective implementation of proven quality principles and techniques [that] aims for virtually error free business performance" (2003, p. 3). As a matter of fact, with its application, a company can expect the occurrence of at most 3.4 defects per million opportunities (DPMO), thereby adapting to increasing consumer expectations and product and process complexity.

In order to achieve such results, Six Sigma relies on its Define-Measure-Analyze-Improve-Control (DMAIC) model, which intends to:

- Define the goals of the improvement activity;
- Measure the existing system;
- Analyze the system to identify ways to eliminate the gap between the current performance of the system or process and the desired goal;
- Improve the system; and
- Control the new system (Pyzdek, 2003, p. 4).

This model can be represented as in Figure 13.

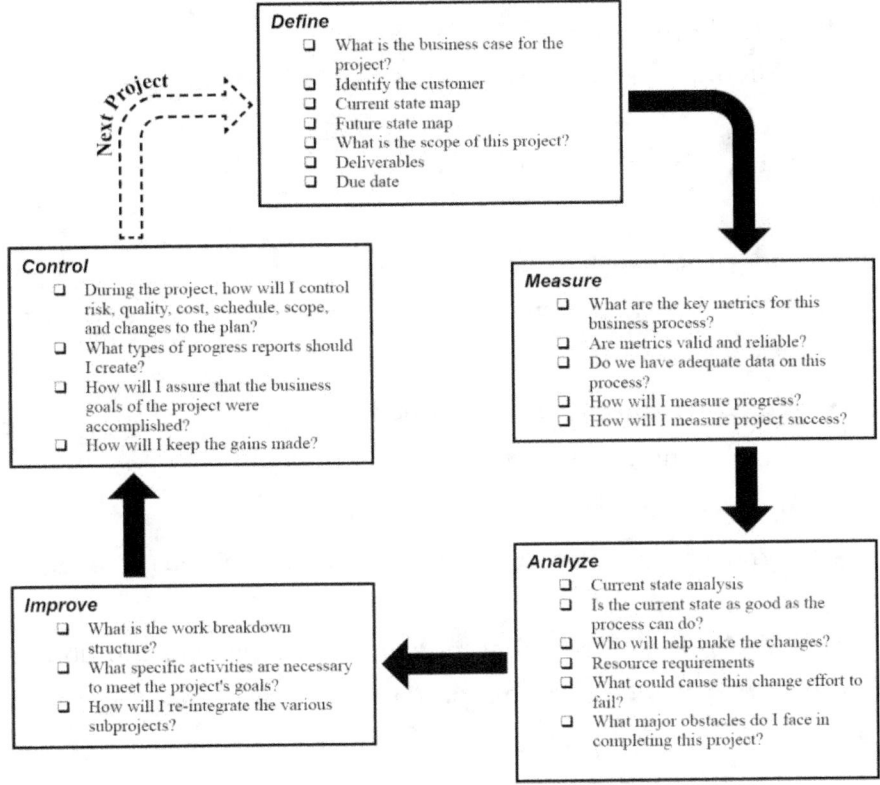

Figure 13. Six Sigma DMAIC

Source: Pyzdek (2003, p. 239)

II.2.2.8. Effective Meetings

Since the amount and frequency of meetings increase with outsourcing, these should be held in the most efficient manner, also because time costs. In this sense, Gerwick (2013, p. 176) highlights and suggests the:

- Distribution of a structured agenda, so that participants can prepare properly for the meeting;
- Establishment of ground rules and time limits for agenda items;

- Enforcement of etiquette rules; and
- Mindfulness of the participants' time and input.

Similarly, Hartman (2014) offers a few tips:

- State the meeting's objective clearly;
- Consider who is invited;
- Stick to the schedule;
- Interrupt conversation monopolizers;
- Start on time, end on time;
- Ban technology; and
- Send a follow-up memo within 24 hours after the meeting.

Meanwhile, Emily Axelrod, according to an anonymous contributor to the Leader to Leader magazine (How To Make Meetings More Effective, 2015), advises to:

- Determine if [the] meeting is really necessary;
- Develop a meaningful purpose that is clear, understood, and accepted by everyone present;
- Make sure the decision makers are present;
- Involve participants in the design of the meeting;
- Ensure that how decisions will be made is clear at the start of the decision-making process;
- Build [the] meeting so that autonomy, meaning, challenge, learning, and feedback are present;
- Treat all participants as if they were volunteers; better yet make all [the] meetings voluntary; [and]
- Be prepared to offer first aid.

In addition to seeking ways to contribute to the meeting's success, as a participant.

CHAPTER III
METHODOLOGICAL
FRAMEWORK

This chapter succinctly describes how this field project was executed, indicating the type of study, the investigation methodology followed, and how the proposed toolkit was prepared.

III.1. Type of Study

This field project is based on a qualitative research, consisting of a literature review and an empirical analysis, regarding the identification of the main issues that hinder outsourcing endeavors and the methodologies, frameworks, tools, and techniques that might help prevent such problems.

III.2. Investigation Methodology

The qualitative research consisted of a literature review, followed by an empirical analysis.

III.2.1. Literature Review

The literature review presented in Chapter II helped identify the key concepts for the comprehension of this document and the topic at hand; presented eight recent unsuccessful outsourcing case studies, which illustrate in a more tangible manner the main issues that hinder this kind of endeavor; and continued with the methodologies, frameworks, tools, and techniques that might help prevent such problems, including ISO 37500:2014.

As of the sources, although books, research papers, magazines, and websites were consulted, precedence was given to the first couple over the latter, where possible, to offer a more solid foundation, from a scientific point of view.

III.2.2. Empirical Analysis

As of the empirical analysis, several semi-structured interviews were conducted face-to-face with local participants and over the phone with those abroad. However, the meetings with senior managers and executives abroad were held more formally, by making a first contact, during which a brief description of this research was provided, setting up phone call appointments, and conducting the interviews in a concise and focused manner, with particular concern for the participants' limited availability. Therefore, most conversations didn't last more than 30 minutes.

Regarding semi-structured interviews, they require the preparation of a number of "sufficiently open" questions in advance, to be asked in the first (structured) part of the conversation, while setting up the stage for the second (unstructured or open) part, during which supplementary improvised questions are asked "in a careful and theorized way" (Wengraf, 2001, p. 5). In other words, this kind of interview combines "both open-ended and more theoretically driven questions, eliciting data grounded in the experience of the participant as well as data guided by existing constructs in the particular discipline within which one is conducting research" (Galletta, 2013, p. 45). Moreover, the author's experience and knowledge came in handy during the second part, in the sense that the questions were both practically and theoretically driven.

III.2.2.1. Sample Selection

The research sample consisted of thirty-two university graduate professionals, who were selected using the convenience and snowball sampling strategies. In layman's terms, most participants were chosen "conveniently" because they were at the author's reach, either in person (in Milan, Italy) or via phone calls, while a few were "snowballed" by other participants or author's acquaintances, meaning that they referred the author to additional participants.

As of the sample's composition, the interviewees worked on the client's or provider's side, occupied positions ranging from consultant to vice-president at 19 different companies at the time of the interview, and were located in America (2), Asia (1), and Europe (29). Of these, one was a vice-president, one an associate director, another one an entrepreneur, seven were project managers, and twenty-two were intermediate to senior level employees. Thirty worked for companies in the ICT sector, one for company in manufacturing, and another for one in the banking sector. Half are men, half are women, with ages ranging between 27 and 58 years, and the average lying at 34 years. Their work experience oscillated between 3 and 34 years, with a mean of 8 years.

Furthermore, the author was included as one of the participants, because his experience was deemed relevant for this research's purposes. However, no specific distinctions were made among the participants, as well as the author, to preserve their anonymity and prevent the association of their answers with the companies for which they worked or to which they provided services.

III.2.2.2. Questionnaire

Table 4 shows the questionnaire used throughout the first part of the interviews.

Table 4. Interview Questionnaire

#	Question
1	How do you feel about your outsourcing experience on the [client's or provider's] side?
2	How would you describe your counterpart?
3	Can you think of some aspects that could be improved?
4	Did you notice or experience any adversities?
5	Did you use a particular methodology, framework, or tool to overcome them?

Source: Prepared by the author

Each question was written and ordered keeping in mind the first and second specific objectives of this research. Evidently, follow-up questions were asked where deemed appropriate and the second part of the interview took these answers into consideration.

III.2.3. Qualitative Data Collection and Analysis

After briefly analyzing each case study, the main adversities and their causes were included in a master table.

During the interviews, the author jotted down the most relevant points, without mentioning people or company names, thus preserving their anonymity. Interestingly, when the author mentioned a theoretical or empirical example after listening to the participants' answers, it motivated them to open up and contribute with more significant answers. Therefore, the interviews weren't plain Q&A sessions, but rather dialogues. After the initial filter in situ, the responses were analyzed, summarized and organized into groups. Subsequently, the findings were listed and discussed in Chapter IV.

III.2.4. Proposed Toolkit

The toolkit proposed in Chapter V was written taking into account the available theory, the results of the case studies identified in the literature review, the findings of the empirical analysis, and the author's experience.

As of its structure, Subchapter V.0, *Before Even Thinking About Outsourcing*, is meant to send a clear message to the reader regarding the importance of a formal organizational model and the identification of non-core functional areas and processes. Specifically, this should prevent situations like those in Case 5 and Case 6 from happening.

Skipping the introduction, Subchapter V.2 presents three modelling tools and techniques that should help to better represent, understand, and improve roles, flows, and processes, such as those related to performance monitoring or issue escalation. An incremental example was developed throughout these sections.

Successively, Subchapter V.3, *Access Control*, refers to the extra hours situation and how these may be extracted from the access control systems currently available at most large companies.

Afterwards, Subchapter V.4, *External Employee Access*, takes care of the work environment circumstances, by providing a list of activities to complete when expecting a provider's employee at the client's site.

Then, the PMBoK Guide, ITIL, Six Sigma are presented to aid the client in managing projects, services, or increasing quality levels, respectively.

Finally, the client is encouraged to introduce a clause regarding prizes and penalties in the contract, benchmark continually the costs of its insourced and outsourced processes and activities with respect to the market, and prepare for an eventual backsourcing process.

CHAPTER IV
RESULTS

Having completed the interviews, this chapter begins with a few considerations, then presents the main findings, and finishes with their brief discussion, one by one.

IV.1. Initial Considerations

Since the sample was heavily biased towards intermediate to senior level employees, the participants' responses were expected to be more related to the operational matters of outsourcing than to strategic or tactical topics. Nevertheless, the semi-structured interviews turned out to be more beneficial than expected, as the open part offered the flexibility required to communicate with participants at any of these three levels, without missing any meaningful information.

IV.2. Main Findings

The main findings that emerged from the interviews were:

1. On the client's side, the people involved in outsourcing ventures usually add this responsibility to those of their full-time jobs;

2. Too many long, ineffective, and inefficient meetings are being held;
3. Some providers seemed to have backstage unethical behaviors;
4. Several provider's employees aren't motivated;
5. There are no client-provider integration events; and
6. The client didn't appropriately prepare for outsourcing.

IV.2.1. Responsibility Overload

Participants on the client's side indicated that, before they were involved in outsourcing ventures, they already had their hands full with work and that, rather than replacing a few of their previous responsibilities, they had to take on those of outsourcing. An interviewee suggested that companies should have people dedicating 80-100% of their time to outsourcing activities.

IV.2.2. Meetings

With follow-up questions, the interviewees further described the ineffective meetings:

- Meetings are set at the last minute;
- People arrive late;
- The speakers don't prepare well nor focus on the purpose of the meeting;
- Someone always asks a question that's unrelated to the meeting and the speaker deviates from the topic at hand;
- A listener is given the task of taking notes and then preparing and sending minutes to the participants —nobody likes doing this;
- Some listeners get distracted and miss the core of the meeting;

- Most of the meeting doesn't concern all the listeners;
- The meeting could've been held via chat or e-mail.

Considering the first finding, since most meeting participants have a very limited availability, meetings should be held in the most efficient and effective manner.

IV.2.3. Backstage Unethical Behavior

The author was surprised when a participant on the provider's side pointed out that his boss had asked him to work on a project for a client and fake being a colleague who held a higher position in the company. Apparently, the boss' reasoning was that, since the client had never seen the colleague, the client wouldn't find out. Fruitfully, when this was mentioned anonymously to another interviewee, he provided a feasible solution: to include a clause in the contract allowing unannounced visits to the provider's workplace. In fact, in a successive interview, having brought up this solution as an example, a different participant on the provider's side remembered an announced visit to the headquarters. She revealed that, the day before, the bosses asked the workers to adopt a certain dress code and behavior, just for that visit.

Another shady situation regarded the provider charging the client for consultants that weren't working, or never worked, on the services offered, thereby inflating prices. This might be indirectly considered a "no-show job." A participant on the client's side suggested brief periodic check-up meetings with the provider's employees, to verify their knowledge of, and involvement in, the outsourced activities. An interviewee on the provider's side offered a different solution: simply have the consultants work at the client's site.

Along the same lines, a participant illustrated how a shared service turned out to be one person (him) supporting eight different clients from the provider's headquarters.

Most participants on the provider's side indicated that they work at least 10 hours a day, yet don't insert them in their time sheets. After further questioning, a couple of reasons emerged: they didn't know they had the right to be paid for the extra hours or their bosses told them not to insert them in their time sheets and that, if they did, their bosses still wouldn't pay for them. However, the client is certainly paying for them.

Furthermore, several interviewees (on both sides) talked about "fixed" résumés. The idea behind this is to make a provider's employee more appealing to the client during the vendor selection phase, by "tweaking" their résumés by adding competences or work experience. Some proposed to look at the candidates' professional networking profiles and perform a cross-check.

Last but not least, a participant pointed out how the "everyone does everything" approach made it much harder for the client to calculate how much work each consultant was doing and "if they were getting what they paid for." Moreover, several participants on the provider's side stated that, while being at one client's site, they dedicated part of their work time to projects or services for other clients. A participant mentioned the introduction of a proxy server to block connections to other systems and websites. However, by using VPN connections, which aren't blocked by most clients, users can skip the proxy filters and easily access other systems.

IV.2.4. Lack of Motivation

Several provider employees added that their companies didn't show much interest in helping them grow professionally. Some were assigned to projects just because someone else was needed, without much concern for their capabilities and interests.

Others felt that they were overqualified for the job and the company didn't appreciate it. They kept going to work because they needed the money and hadn't found a work opportunity elsewhere.

A few indicated that there's a rule at the client's canteen, according to which the providers' employees are only admitted after 2:00 PM for lunch, and that the meals cost them much more than for the client's employees.

Some mentioned that there's a significant difference between what they're being paid and what the company charges for their services.

Most of these issues could be associated to the case study about Organization X (see II.2.1.7), which at some point discussed employee benefits and work conditions (Cabral, Quelin, & Maia, 2014, p. 369).

IV.2.5. Client-Provider Integration

Several participants further indicated that both parties usually meet when they need something from each other, but the relationship doesn't go beyond. Some people pass by each other, day after day, for years and still haven't met. In fact, the workplace is a second home for most people and they should feel welcomed, not isolated. Integration events would certainly help.

Evidently, this hinders client-provider collaboration and significant trust levels aren't reached.

IV.2.6. Unprepared Client

Unfortunately, in a few cases the clients didn't prepare well for the outsourcing venture. For example, during the delivery phase, the client asked the provider to propose a procedure, according to which it's performance would be monitored, and to recommend a set of KPIs to observe.

In other cases, it surfaced that employees of several clients didn't have a relevant academic preparation which would've helped them gain a better understanding of the matter at hand, guide and support their decisions, estimate the costs of activities with more precision, assess the respective risks, evaluate the provider's performance more accurately, know the tips and tricks of the art and which approaches to enforce or discourage, and contribute to the preparation of an ideally ironclad contract.

Many participants on the provider's side brought up space and work environment considerations at the client's site. Some had to search for chairs every day, since there weren't enough for everyone. An interviewee had to sit on the staircase, on a few occasions, because he couldn't find one. Others were crammed up due to the lack of desks. In some cases, employees of different providers were assigned to the same rooms. There was no place to make business phone calls, so most talked in the hallways. Some reported difficulties in using meeting rooms, because in several client sites the external employees weren't given access to the meeting room booking system, so they entered when the rooms were empty, but left when other people came. Evidently, meetings couldn't be efficiently scheduled nor held.

CHAPTER V
TOOLKIT

V.0. Before Even Thinking About Outsourcing

Before even thinking about outsourcing, the client-to-be should have already developed a model of its organizational structure, including formal functional area and role descriptions; defined a sourcing strategy; determined which are the company's core functional areas and processes; and which non-core functional area or process to outsource, in addition to its performance indicators and cost.

If even one of these aspects were missing, the client would be highly advised to address them before even thinking about outsourcing.

V.1. Introduction

This toolkit responds to the adversities that emerged from the analysis of eight case studies and thirty-two field interviews and was designed to be used in conjunction with the ISO 37500:2014. It begins by proposing a set of role, flow, and process modelling tools and techniques, while carrying on an example that is then used when referring to an access control mechanism. Afterwards, several considerations on external employee access to the client's site are discussed, tips on effective meetings are offered, checkup meetings are presented as workplace sonars, unannounced visits are emphasized, and integration events are advertised. Subsequently, the PMBoK Guide, ITIL, and Six Sigma are introduced as possible solutions to project management, IT service management, and quality-related issues, with bonus/malus measures. Finally, continual benchmarking and backsourcing preparedness are discussed.

V.2. Modelling Tools and Techniques

This subchapter contains three modelling tools and techniques meant to help identify and describe roles, flows, and processes and effectively communicate them to other stakeholders.

V.2.1. UML Use Case Diagrams

Although UML use case diagrams are generally used to illustrate what a specific kind of user can do with a system, in the outsourcing context it may also be used to represent the actions expected from individuals occupying a particular role, throughout a certain activity. For instance, Figure 14 depicts what a provider's employee could do at the client's site.

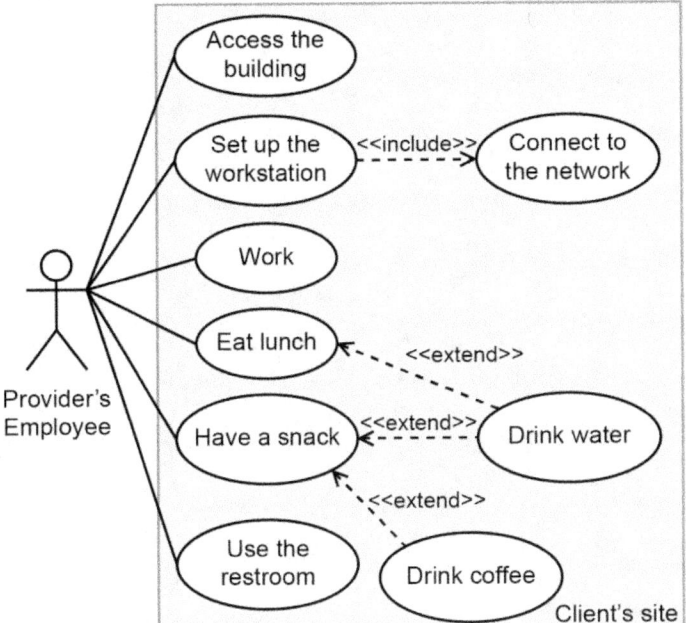

Figure 14. Provider's Employee at the Client's Site Use Case Diagram
Source: Prepared by the author

Even though this is an extremely simple example, it should demonstrate how this kind of diagram could easily be understood by anyone. Additionally, a brief description is usually included, indicating the details of each use case.

V.2.2. Flowcharts

Flowcharts are good representations of flows or sequences of activities or tasks, where no distinction is made about who, or what, is executing them. In this sense, it might come in handy when delving into a particular use case. Reconsidering the "Access the building" use case, the diagram in Figure 15 was generated.

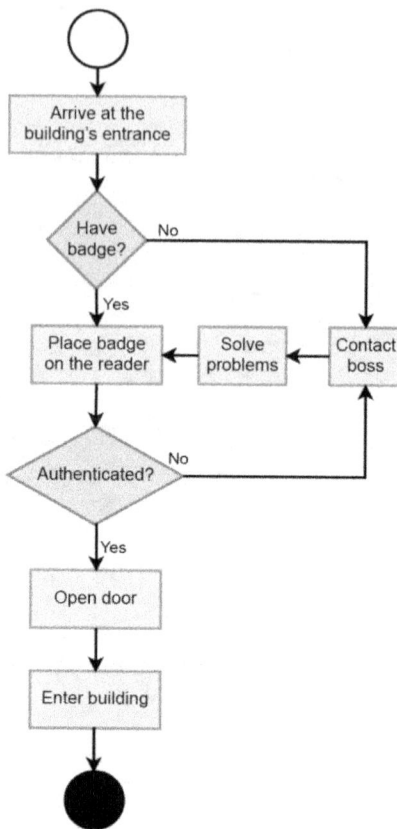

Figure 15. Building Access Flowchart Diagram
Source: Prepared by the author

As can be seen, when multiple agents or roles are involved, the diagram becomes ambiguous. In this trivial case, for example, who solves the problems? Who or what opens the door? Although these questions could be answered in the accompanying prosaic document, the appropriate type of diagram would transmit this data in an instant.

V.2.3. Business Process Modeling Notation (BPMN)

In cases where several participants, departments, or systems are involved, like in the previous one, it's better to use Business Process

Modeling Notation (BPMN) diagrams.

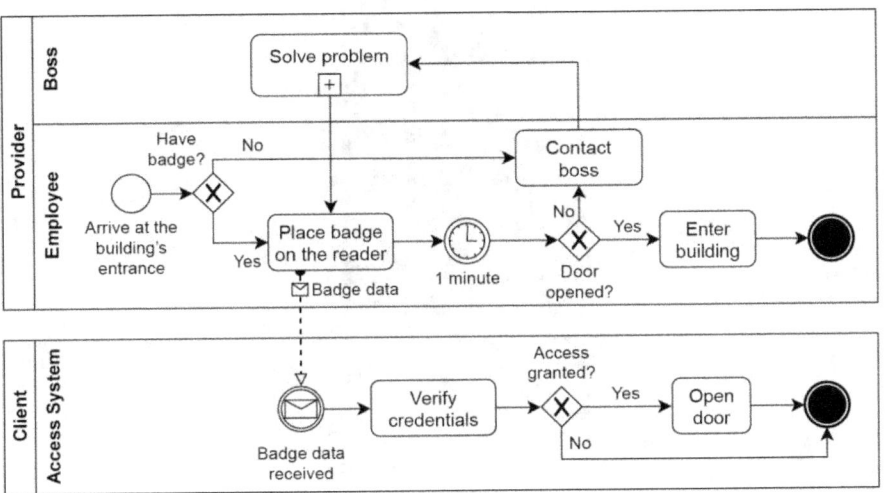

Figure 16. Building Access BPMN Diagram

Source: Prepared by the author

Indisputably, this is the most complex of all three types of diagram and consequently takes more time to elaborate. Therefore, it should be used for the aforementioned purposes and not as a replacement of the other two when less details are required.

V.3. Access Control

Since employee access control to buildings is nowadays performed mostly via software (Figure 16) and hardware (Figure 17), clients with this kind of system can easily generate reports on the number of hours worked by their internal and external personnel, including extra hours.

Figure 17. Electronic Time Card

Source: Zucchetti s.p.a. (n.d.)

V.4. External Employee Access

Before the arrival of a provider's employee, the client should make sure that this person has the credentials necessary to access the building and work area, that there's an adequate workspace available, with all the required furniture, equipment, cables, and network and software access codes. The external employee should also read a purposefully prepared workplace hazards brochure for this specific client, who usually requires a signature confirming having read it. However, most people sign the form without ever opening the brochure.

Meeting rooms and call booths should also be stipulated, in addition to a booking system or mechanism.

V.5. Meetings, Visits, and Events

This subchapter presents techniques meant to reduce cost and time waste; detect overprepared, oversold, unmotivated, "no-show," and "no-work" employees; and raise trust and collaboration levels.

V.5.1. Effective Meetings

To keep the governance overhead that results from outsourcing at its minimum, meetings should be as effective and efficient as possible. In this sense, the following list offers tips on how to achieve this goal:

1. Delineate a clear objective;
2. Determine if the meeting is necessary or if other means could be used;
3. Consider whom to invite: attendees should be present only when the topic concerns them or their input might be valuable;
4. Calculate the cost of the meeting;
5. Create and share a prioritized meeting agenda with enough anticipation, containing a time limit for each of its items;
6. Start on time, end on time;
7. Set the ground rules, including a technology ban;
8. Make announcements right before the end, never at the beginning;
9. Keep the meeting focused and on time;
10. Follow up by sending the minutes within the 24 hours.

Figure 18 indicates how to calculate a meeting's cost.

SIDEBAR
CALCULATING THE COST OF A STAFF MEETING

20
Number of people attending the staff meeting
×

$65.95 ($33.65 + $32.30) per hour for each staff member
Total compensation package of the group divided to determine an hourly wage
(Allot $5.00 for every $10,000 in annual compensation package per nurse)
×

2
Number of hours the meeting runs
+

$200.00
Preparation and planning time
($100.00 for each hour the meeting is expected to run)
=

$2,838.00
Total expense of a 2-hour staff meeting
(This figure does not include the cost of work that is not getting done while staff
members attend a meeting.)

Note. The staff nurse's salary is based on the national median salary for RNs in the United States = $64,600
(Davis, 2009; U.S. News and World Report, 2012).

Figure 18. Calculating the Cost of a Staff Meeting
Source: Gerwick (2013, p. 174)

V.5.2. Checkup Meetings

Random one-to-one checkup meetings with the provider's personnel at the client's site might help detect unmotivated employees, better evaluate their qualifications (check for overqualified or oversold workers), determine the provider's proclivity for innovation (technology, research, and professional growth investments), and open a space for suggestions and improvement ideas. Furthermore, they might also help uncover no-show and no-work employees. Both an HR representative and a functional representative should be present to evaluate workers from both sides.

For the same reasons, a checkup meeting should also be held before the provider's employee starts working for the client.

Therefore, the topics discussed, and questions asked, during these meetings should be planned ahead, not improvised.

V.5.3. Unannounced Visits

The client should always stipulate a clause in the outsourcing contract allowing unannounced visits to all the provider's sites. This way, by showing up without warning, a client's committee can verify the provider's work conditions and that the personnel that's being paid for is actually there. It might also be convenient to carry out checkup meetings with them, then and there, for the aforementioned reasons.

V.5.4. Integration Events

Well planned integration events, where everyone is introduced, usually raise the trust levels, create a warm and welcoming environment at the workplace, and enhance client-provider collaboration.

V.6. Projects with the PMBoK Guide

If the outsourcing endeavor comprises projects, the Project Management Body of Knowledge (PMBoK) Guide is highly advised, as it delves into all standard aspects and best practices of project management in a very comprehensible manner and its layout is very similar to that of the ISO 37500:2014, in addition to being internationally recognized in multiple industries.

Focusing on its application to outsourcing, different aspects could be organized and managed as projects. In fact, the Project Management Institute (PMI) defines a project as "a temporary endeavor undertaken to create a unique product, service, or result" (2017, p. 4). An example could be the development of a software tool to support the vendor vetting (selection) process. This tool could also be subject to outsourcing, in the sense that the entire development project, or parts of it, could be outsourced, with the appropriate considerations. In all cases, the PMBoK Guide should be the starting and main reference point when pondering projects of any kind, even those somehow related to outsourcing.

Said guide also provides a varied set of tools and techniques that could be applied widely, not just to projects. A few of these are: multicriteria decision analysis, brainstorming, focus groups, histograms, Ishikawa (fishbone) diagrams, and responsible-accountable-consulted-informed (RACI) charts.

As of project management software solutions, some of the most popular are Microsoft Project, Atlassian JIRA, Trello, and CA Clarity PPM.

V.7. Services with ITIL

If instead, or additionally, the outsourcing venture regarded IT services, the client might benefit from the Information Technology Infrastructure Library (ITIL), which is widely recognized as a best practice in the IT industry. In fact, both parties (i.e. client and provider) usually base several of their activities on ITIL and even take into account certain of its aspects when writing outsourcing contracts. For instance, service-level agreement (SLA) clauses are commonly included in contracts of this kind and are subsequently monitored via ticket, help desk, or service desk management systems, such as Altiris, HP Service Manager, Remedy, and SysAid.

V.8. Quality with Six Sigma

Although both the PMBoK Guide and ITIL provide quality assurance and control techniques, Six Sigma focuses on quality and process improvement and is applicable to multiple industries. By applying the Define-Measure-Analyze-Improve-Control (DMAIC) model and using specific Six Sigma tools and software solutions, such as Minitab and Microsoft Excel + SigmaXL, to assist with calculations, the process error rates could be significantly reduced and so could the process variation, hence obtaining a consistent result almost all the time.

In this sense, Six Sigma could be applied to outsourcing processes, like those described in the ISO 37500, expecting to achieve greater levels of efficiency and constancy, while guaranteeing a continuous and competitive process evolution. Moreover, its combination with the previously described modelling tools and the PMBoK Guide or ITIL will hopefully lead to a greater outsourcing success rate.

V.9. Bonus/malus

Talking about quality, bonus and malus clauses should be added to the contract, to premiate or penalize the provider, according to its timeliness, quality, and performance. In this respect, the PMBoK Guide, ITIL, and Six Sigma should help identify the appropriate indicators and stipulate the respective processes and procedures to monitor and control them.

V.10. Continual Benchmarking

The client should continually benchmark the cost of its insourced and outsourced activities with the market and be on the lookout for strategic opportunities. For a period, it might be convenient to perform certain activities inhouse. Yet, after a game-changing event (e.g. new technologies, competitors, laws, free trade agreements, or political ideologies), outsourcing could be the way to go. Or vice-versa, from outsourcing to backsourcing.

V.11. Always Be Prepared to Backsource

Therefore, the possibility of backsourcing should be considered as early as possible, in order to insert adequate clauses in the outsourcing contract to make an eventual termination as smooth as possible. Also, if firing or transferring personnel to the provider, it is suggested to keep the key figures when outsourcing. Case studies show that this makes a significant difference when backsourcing. Moreover, the client should foresee a backsourcing point that allows it to recover from a failed outsourcing endeavor and still offer a desirable product/service to the market.

CONCLUSIONS

Having started with the description and contextualization of the problem on which this research focused, a set of objectives aimed at its solution were proposed, taking into account specific assumptions, delimitations, and limitations, hoping to achieve what was stated as the justification of this work.

Successively, a reference framework was built, beginning with several concepts that were deemed necessary for the comprehension of this document and were contextualized to its scope, while being complementary to those defined in the ISO 37500:2014 and common to the outsourcing jargon. Afterwards, the theoretical framework was presented, including the description of eight recent case studies and the methodologies, frameworks, tools, and techniques extracted from theory that were later incorporated into the toolkit.

Subsequently, the methodology followed throughout this research was described, regarding both the literature review and empirical analysis, the former of which consisted of the elaboration of the reference framework. As of the latter, numerous interviews were carried on with the purpose of identifying experiential and practical elements that could further contribute to this study. Then, an explanation of how each section of the toolkit addresses the adversities extracted from the literature review and empirical analysis was provided.

Next, the results of the interviews were listed by groups, each of which was discussed separately. In particular, the composition of the sample was highly relevant to the kind of results obtained, in the sense that most of the responses were related to the operational level, which is in line with the sample mainly consisting of intermediate to senior level employees.

Finally, the toolkit was proposed as a means to avoid or prevent the appearance of the unnecessary adversities derived from, and revealed by, the literature review and empirical analysis. Specifically, three modeling tools and techniques were presented with the purpose of helping identify and describe roles, flows, and processes and effectively communicate them to other stakeholders; several considerations on external employee access to the client's site were discussed; a few techniques meant to reduce cost and time waste, detect overprepared, oversold, unmotivated, "no-show," and "no-work" employees, and raise trust and collaboration levels were recommended; the PMBoK Guide was proposed as the starting and main reference point for projects of any kind; similarly, the ITIL for IT services and Six Sigma for quality assurance and control, to be accompanied by bonus/malus clauses. The toolkit closes by emphasizing the importance of continually benchmarking the insourced and outsourced activities with the market, while remaining on the lookout for strategic opportunities, in addition to always being prepared to backsource.

Hopefully, also the reader benefitted from this research and will begin, or continue, avoiding unnecessary adversities.

RECOMMENDATIONS

Considering the aforementioned limitations of this field project (i.e. time, author's work experience, fields of knowledge, location, and composition and reach of his social and work networks), most of which highly influenced and conditioned the selection of the sample for the semi-structured interviews and how they were conducted, future research in this field might regard hosting interviews in other contexts with participants from multiple countries, holding positions at the strategic or tactical level, in order to study this matter from more perspectives.

Since this toolkit wasn't tested, as stated previously, the results of its application, or of its parts, might also be a starting point for successive research. In particular, further analysis of the combination of the PMBoK guide, ITIL, and Six Sigma with the ISO 37500 might result in meaningful contributions to this field.

LIST OF REFERENCES

Bort, J. (2013, December 6). *IBM Sued Over $1 Billion Project That Led To It Being Banned By Queensland, Australia.* Retrieved from Business Insider: https://www.businessinsider.com/queensland-sues-ibm-over-1b-project-2013-12

Cabral, S., Quelin, B., & Maia, W. (2014). Outsourcing Failure and Reintegration: The Influence of Contractual and External Factors. *Long Range Planning, 47*(6), 365-378.

Chakrabarty, S. (2007). Strategies for Business Process Outsourcing: An Analysis of Alternatives, Opportunities, and Risks. In J. Sounderpandian, & T. Sinha, *E-Business Process Management: Technologies and Solutions* (pp. 204-229). Hershey, PA: Idea Group Publishing. doi:10.4018/978-1-59904-204-6.ch011

Chesterman, R. N. (2013). *Queensland Health Payroll System Commission of Inquiry - Report.* Retrieved October 27, 2018, from http://www.healthpayrollinquiry.qld.gov.au/__data/assets/pdf_file/0014/207203/Queensland-Health-Payroll-System-Commission-of-Inquiry-Report-31-July-2013.pdf

Core Process. (n.d.). Retrieved October 7, 2018, from BusinessDictionary: http://www.businessdictionary.com/definition/core-process.html

Cowan, P. (2016, June 20). *Queensland's IBM ban lives on.* Retrieved

from itnews:
https://www.itnews.com.au/news/queenslands-ibm-ban-lives-on-420969

Davenport, T. H. (1993). The Nature of Process Innovation. In *Process innovation: reengineering work through information technology* (pp. 1-21). Boston: Harvard Business School Press.

Dumas, M., La Rosa, M., Mendling, J., & Reijers, H. A. (2018). Introduction to Business Process Management. In *Fundamentals of Business Process Management* (2 ed., pp. 1-33). Springer. doi:10.1007/978-3-662-56509-4

EBA European Banking Authority. (2018, June 22). Consultation Paper - EBA Draft Guidelines on Outsourcing Arrangements. Retrieved October 14, 2018, from https://www.eba.europa.eu/documents/10180/2260326/Consultation+Paper+on+draft+Guidelines+on+outsourcing+arrangements+%28EBA-CP-2018-11%29.pdf

Feldmann, U., Leak, S. G., & Hendrichs, J. (2018). Assessing the feasibility of creating tsetse and trypanosomosis-free zones. *International Journal of Tropical Insect Science, 38*(1), 77–92. doi:10.1017/S1742758417000285

flowchart. (n.d.). Retrieved November 4, 2018, from SEVOCAB: Software and Systems Engineering Vocabulary: https://pascal.computer.org/sev_display/index.action

Galletta, A. (2013). The Semi-Structured Interview as a Repertoire of Possibilities. In *Mastering the Semi-Structured Interview and Beyond: From Research Design to Analysis and Publication* (pp. 45-72). New York: New York University Press.

Garland, A. (2015, December 19). *Five of the biggest outsourcing failures.* Retrieved from ITProPortal: https://www.itproportal.com/2015/12/19/five-of-the-biggest-outsourcing-failures/

Gerwick, M. A. (2013). Strategies for Effective Meetings. *Journal of continuing education in nursing,* 1-7.

Gilley, K. M., & Rasheed, A. (2000). Making More by Doing Less:

An Analysis of Outsourcing and its Effects on Firm Performance. *Journal of Management, 26*(4), 763-790.

Govindarajan, V. (2012, April 16). *P&G Innovates on Razor-Thin Margins*. Retrieved from Harvard Business Review: https://hbr.org/2012/04/how-pg-innovates-on-razor-thin

Harland, C., Knight, L., Lamming, R., & Walker, H. (2005). Outsourcing: assessing the risks and benefits for organisations, sectors and nations. *International Journal of Operations & Production Management, 25*(9), 831-850. doi:10.1108/01443570510613929

Harmon, P. (2014). Understanding and Scoping Process. In P. Harmon, *Business Process Change* (pp. 185-209). Morgan Kaufmann.

Hartman, N. (2014, February 5). *Seven Steps to Running the Most Effective Meeting Possible*. Retrieved November 4, 2018, from Forbes: https://www.forbes.com/sites/forbesleadershipforum/2014/02/05/seven-steps-to-running-the-most-effective-meeting-possible/

Hindle, T. (2008). Cannibalisation. In T. Hindle, *Guide to Management Ideas and Gurus* (pp. 27-28). London: Profile Books Ltd.

Hinkelman, E. G. (2008). Guide to International Sourcing (Outsourcing). In *Dictionary of International Trade: Handbook of the Global Trade Community* (pp. 578-602). World Trade Press.

Homeshoring. (n.d.). Retrieved October 14, 2018, from Macmillan Dictionary: https://www.macmillandictionary.com/dictionary/british/homeshoring

How To Make Meetings More Effective. (2015). *Leader to Leader*, 67-68. doi:10.1002/ltl.20181

Intranet Development Project. (n.d.). Retrieved August 29, 2018, from Failing IT Projects: https://www.kellogg.northwestern.edu/student/courses/tech914/summer2004/projectfailures/projectfailures/navy2.htm

ISO. (2014). *International Standard 37500 "Guidance on Outsourcing"*.

Geneva: International Organization for Standardization.

ISO/IEC. (2015). *ISO/IEC 2382:2015(en) Information technology - Vocabulary*. Retrieved from ISO Online Browsing Platform: https://www.iso.org/obp/ui/#iso:std:iso-iec:2382:ed-1:v1:en

ITV. (2018, August 23). *Shopping: End of the High Street? - Tonight*. Retrieved from ITV: http://www.itv.com/news/2018-08-23/shopping-end-of-the-high-street-tonight/

Khalfan, A. (2003). A case analysis of business process outsourcing project failure profile and implementation problems in a large organisation of a developing nation. *Business Process Management Journal, 9*(6), 745-759. doi:10.1108/14637150310506675

Kumar, N. (2003, December). *Kill a Brand, Keep a Customer*. Retrieved from Harvard Business Review: https://hbr.org/2003/12/kill-a-brand-keep-a-customer

Law, F. (2018). Breaking the outsourcing path: Backsourcing process and outsourcing lock-in. *European Management Journal, 36*(3), 341-352. doi:10.1016/j.emj.2017.05.004

Lee, D. (2013). Business Process Management. In T. Benedict, N. Bilodeau, P. Vitkus, E. Powell, D. Morris, M. Scharsig, . . . C. Moore, *BPM CBOK Version 3.0: Guide to the Business Process Management Common Body Of Knowledge* (pp. 39-82). North Charleston: CreateSpace.

LeMay, R. (2010, October 11). *Navitaire outage to cost Virgin $15-20m*. Retrieved October 28, 2018, from Delimiter: https://delimiter.com.au/2010/10/11/navitaire-outage-to-cost-virgin-15-20m/

Lucid Software Inc. (n.d.). *Diagrams for Dummies: A BPMN Tutorial*. Retrieved November 11, 2018, from Lucidchart: https://www.lucidchart.com/blog/diagrams-for-dummies-a-BPMN-tutorial

Lucid Software Inc. (n.d.). *UML Use Case Diagram Tutorial*. Retrieved November 5, 2018, from Lucidchart: https://www.lucidchart.com/pages/uml-use-case-diagram

Lucid Software Inc. (n.d.). *What is Business Process Modeling Notation.* Retrieved November 11, 2018, from Lucidchart: https://www.lucidchart.com/pages/bpmn

Martin, N. (2018, June 18). *As US, UK 'retail apocalypse' deepens, EU chains grow nervous.* Retrieved from Deutsche Welle: https://www.dw.com/en/as-us-uk-retail-apocalypse-deepens-eu-chains-grow-nervous/a-44271346

Most outsourcing failures flawed before they start. (2004, October 21). *Supply Management, 9*(21), 10.

Mullin, R. (1996). Managing the Outsourced Enterprise. *Journal of Business Strategy, 17*(4), 28-36.

Najafi, N., Holmen, E., Lind, F., & Pedersen, A.-C. (2014). Changing sourcing strategies to make the most of them. *IMP Conference.* Bordeaux. Retrieved from https://www.impgroup.org/uploads/papers/8252.pdf

Oates, J. (2004, November 16). *US Navy blows $375m hole in EDS accounts.* Retrieved October 27, 2018, from The Register: https://www.theregister.co.uk/2004/11/16/usnavy_hits_eds/

Outsource. (n.d.). Retrieved October 13, 2018, from Oxford Dictionaries: https://en.oxforddictionaries.com/definition/us/outsource

Parniangtong, S. (2016). Strategic Sourcing: Concepts, Principles and Methodology. In *Supply Management: Strategic Sourcing* (pp. 5-14). Springer. doi:10.1007/978-981-10-1723-0

Project Management Institute. (2017). *A guide to the project management body of knowledge (PMBOK guide)* (6th ed.). Newton Square, PA: Project Management Institute, Inc.

Prystupa, K., & Rządca, M. (2015). Outsourcing Failures In SME's: Case Study Approach. *Problems of Management in the 21st Century*, 37-46.

Pyzdek, T. (2003). *The Six Sigma Handbook: The Complete Guide for Greenbelts, Blackbelts, and Managers at All Levels* (2nd ed.). New York, NY: McGraw-Hill. doi:10.1036/0071415963

Reshoring. (n.d.). Retrieved October 14, 2018, from Investopedia: https://www.investopedia.com/terms/r/reshoring.asp

Ritchie, M. (2015, January 6). *Outsourcing's booming business.* Retrieved August 27, 2018, from International Organization for Standardization: https://www.iso.org/news/2015/01/Ref1922.html

Roberto, M. A. (2011, June). Portrait of a Transformation. *Transformational Leadership: How Leaders Change Teams, Companies, and Organizations.* The Teaching Company, LLC.

Rouse, M. (2018, July). *business process outsourcing (BPO).* Retrieved August 27, 2018, from SearchCIO: https://searchcio.techtarget.com/definition/business-process-outsourcing

Schneider, G., & Winters, J. P. (2001). Documenting Use Cases. In *Applying Use Cases: A Practical Guide* (pp. 111-159). Pearson Education. Retrieved from https://www.ibm.com/developerworks/rational/library/content/legacy/parttwo/1000/0670/0670_Schneider_Ch07.pdf

Sen, C., & Smith, N. (2018, July 17). *America Confronts the Retail Apocalypse: A Debate.* Retrieved from Bloomberg: https://www.bloomberg.com/view/articles/2018-07-17/e-commerce-keeps-driving-america-s-retail-apocalypse

SlideModel. (n.d.). *ITIL Service Lifecycle PowerPoint Diagram.* Retrieved November 5, 2018, from SlideModel: https://slidemodel.com/templates/itil-service-lifecycle-powerpoint-diagram/

Sourcingmag.com. (n.d.). *Nearshoring.* Retrieved October 14, 2018, from Sourcingmag.com: https://sourcingmag.com/dictionary/nearshoring/

Stern, S. (2007, July 30). *Coming soon: zero tolerance for outsourcing failure.* Retrieved October 28, 2018, from Financial Times: https://www.ft.com/content/9557c4e2-3eb8-11dc-bfcf-0000779fd2ac

Suchenia, A., & Ligęza, A. (2015). Event anomalies in modeling with

BPMN. *International Journal of Computer Technology and Applications (IJCTA), 6*(5), 789-797.

The Economist. (2005, December 3). Special report: The rise of nearshoring - Outsourcing in eastern europe. *The Economist, 377*(8455), 86. Retrieved from https://0-search-proquest-com.opac.unicatt.it/docview/224027458?accountid=9941

von Scheel, H., von Rosing, M., Fonseca, M., Hove, M., & Foldager, U. (2014). Phase 1: Process Concept Evolution. In M. von Rosing, A.-W. Scheer, & H. von Scheel, *The Complete Business Process Handbook: Body of Knowledge from Process Modeling to BPM, Volume 1* (pp. 1-9). Waltham: Morgan Kaufmann.

Vu, X. T. (2015). *User-centered and Group-based Approach for Social Data Filtering and Sharing.* doi:10.13140/RG.2.1.4506.0642

Wengraf, T. (2001). Interview 'Facts' as Evidence to Support Inferences to Eventual Theorization/Representation Models. In *Qualitative Research Interviewing: Biographic Narrative and Semi-Structured Methods* (pp. 2-15). London: SAGE.

Zucchetti s.p.a. (n.d.). *ETC - Il timbra cartellino a prova di privacy!* Retrieved November 5, 2018, from Zucchetti s.p.a.: http://www.zucchetti.it/website/cms/prodotto/2602-orologi-timbracartellini.html

ABOUT THE AUTHOR

    Vick Pierce Dini is a Systems Engineer with a Master's in Corporate Governance. Throughout the years, he has led several software development and process optimization projects for multiple companies, to increase their competitive advantage by cutting costs, achieving better results, and producing greater value for their stakeholders.